W9-AZP-585

JOHN PAUL II ON SCIENCE AND RELIGION

REFLECTIONS ON THE NEW VIEW FROM ROME

EDITED BY

Robert J. Russell,
William R. Stoeger, S.J.,
and
George V. Coyne

1990

Vatican Observatory Publications

© Copyright 1990 by the VATICAN OBSERVATORY FOUNDATION
Published by the VATICAN OBSERVATORY

Manufactured in the United States of America

Ernan McMullin, "A Common Quest for Understanding," is reprinted with the permission of:
America Press, Inc.
106 West 56th Street
New York, NY 10019
©1989 All Rights Reserved

Distributed (except in Italy and Vatican City State) by:

THE UNIVERSITY OF NOTRE DAME PRESS
Notre Dame, Indiana 46556
USA

Distributed in Italy and the Vatican City State by:

LIBRERIA EDITRICE VATICANA
V-00120 Citta' del Vaticano
Vatican City State

ISBN 0-268-01209-1

CONTENTS

Preface   v

Message of His Holiness John Paul II   xii

RICHARD J. BLACKWELL: Science and Religion: The Papal
Call for an Open Dialogue   1

JOHN B. COBB, JR.: One Step Further   5

AVERY DULLES, S.J.: Science and Theology   9

LINDON EAVES: Autonomy is Not Enough   19

GEORGE F.R. ELLIS: Critique: The Church and the Scientific
Community   23

FANG LI ZHI: Note on the Interface Between Science
and Religion   31

ELIZABETH A. JOHNSON, CSJ: Response to the Message of
John Paul II on the Relationship Between the
Scientific and Religious Cultures of Our Times   37

MALU WA KALENGA: Critique of the Message of His Holiness
Pope John Paul II   42

CARDINAL CARLO MARIA MARTINI: The Church and the
Scientific Communities   49

ERNAN McMULLIN: A Common Quest for Understanding   54

CARL MITCHAM: Signs of Contradiction   59

NANCEY MURPHY: The Message of John Paul II on Science
and the Church: A Response   67

WOLFHART PANNENBERG: Theology and Philosophy in
Interaction with Science: A Response to the Message of
Pope John Paul II on the Occasion of the Newton
Tricentennial in 1987   75

TULLIO REGGE: Comments on "The Church and the Scientific Communities: A Common Quest for Understanding" by His Holiness John Paul II 81

HOLMES ROLSTON, III: Joining Science and Religion 83

ROSEMARY RADFORD REUTHER: Religion and Science in an Unjust World 95

KARL SCHMITZ-MOORMAN: Science and Theology in a Changing Vision of the World: Reading John Paul's Message in Physics, *Philosophy and Theology* 99

THOMAS F. TORRANCE: The Message of John Paul II to Theologians and Scientists Commemorating the Third Centenary of Sir Isaac Newton's *Philosophiae Naturalis Principia Mathematica* 106

CHARLES H. TOWNES: A Response to the Message of John Paul II 113

The Contributors 119

Editorial Comments

All references to the papal message are indicated in the text by the page number in parentheses (M1 to M14) and are taken from the text reprinted herein on the pages following page ix, originally published in *Physics, Philosophy and Theology: A Common Quest for Understanding*, eds. R.J. Russell, W.R. Stoeger and G.V. Coyne (Notre Dame, IN: University of Notre Dame Press, 1988).

For uniformity of style we have adopted herein the word Church (at times Churches) with the initial C capitalized to refer either to one of the Christian communions or to all of them considered together.

PREFACE

In the Fall of 1987 an international research conference was convened at the Vatican Observatory. The purpose of the conference was to explore the current relations between theology and science. Its twenty scholars hoped to move in the direction of establishing a new level of dialogue and mutual understanding between scientists, philosophers, and theologians with the possibility of modifying the theological and scientific perspectives which pervade both the Church and the Academy today. The publication of the resulting conference papers was the occasion of an equally ambitious and challenging papal message on science and religion.

The Pope, through the offices of the Vatican Secretariate of State, called for the conference. Even as Archbishop of Krakow, the man who was to be the first Polish Pope was deeply intrigued by questions, not only of religion and politics, but also of cosmology, philosophy, and metaphysics. Then as Pontiff in 1983, in his first serious move to enhance relations between the Church and the scientific community, John Paul took action to overcome the long-lasting effects of the infamous castigation of Galileo Galilei. In a message commemorating the 350th anniversary of the publication of Galileo's _Dialogues_, the Pope indicated that through "humble and assiduous study" the church can begin to "dissociate the essentials of faith from the scientific systems of a given age..." In 1984 a statement was released by the Vatican which admitted that "Church officials had erred in condemning Galileo."[1] But there was more to accomplish for this Pope, much more. Not only should former encroachments be rescinded; a mere sterile truce, a "two worlds" strategy, was not acceptable either. Instead, the theological implications of the natural sciences needed to be clearly and imaginatively confronted.

There are, of course, revolutionary discoveries in the biological sciences and the unsettling technologies flowing from them, which raise critical issues in the philosophy and theology of nature and in philosophical and theological anthropology, as well as in ethics and moral theology. The focus of this conference, however, was directed to the physical sciences, which constitute an often mute but very formidable backdrop for the biological and psychological sciences and about which theologians had been relatively silent for centuries. Could the breathtaking discoveries of our era – the revolutions in our view of space, time, matter and causality, and the panorama of nature ranging from the mysterious world of the atom to the beginning and far future of the universe as a whole – could these be properly and judiciously imported across the theological horizon and then be discussed responsibly within the theological mainstream?

v

Along a different but related vein, major developments have occurred within philosophy this century, including positivism, constructivism, linguistic analysis, post-modernism, new philosophies of time and becoming and the sustained articulation of critical realism. In particular, philosophy of science and philosophy of religion have undergone significant shifts in their discussions about epistemology and methodology. What then is the most fruitful role for philosophy in mediating the interaction of theology and science? How might it help articulate a scientifically informed philosophy of nature?

It was to these and other enormously important questions that the Pope now turned. The occasion was the tricentennial commemoration of the publication of Sir Isaac Newton's *Philosophiae Naturalis Principia Mathematica*. In honor of this occasion John Paul II, through the Vatican Secretariate of State, asked the Director of the Vatican Observatory, Reverend Dr. George V. Coyne, S.J., to convene a top level research conference on physics, philosophy, and theology. The resulting essays are contained in the conference volume, *Physics, Philosophy and Theology: A Common Quest for Understanding.*[2]

But perhaps more important than these essays the volume contains a papal message conveyed as a letter to the Reverend Coyne on the occasion of the publication of the conference volume. This message is unique in that it is the first major papal statement in almost four decades specifically focused on the substantive and constructive relation of theology and science. In it the Pope calls for theologians to take science with extreme seriousness by integrating the results of science into their own theological agendas, holding up Thomas Aquinas himself as a benchmark to surpass. The Pope calls for a new movement towards "unity with integrity" between the Church and the scientific communities, a movement which can overcome fragmentation between those who search for truth in the depths of human experience and history, and those who search for truth in the mysteries of nature. It is a unity which, while ever receding beyond our grasp, beckons us onwards in service and in mutual learning. It is a union based not on assertion but on openness, not on domination but on humility. It is a union based on love.

It is my belief that the papal message deserves an audience of its own. Its destiny should not be linked solely to the conference volume cited above. It deserves a broader hearing and it warrants a direct response from theologians, scientists, and philosophers who can assess its value as a papal pronouncement on an issue facing us all: the future relationship between the Church and the scientific community. Hence the origin of this present volume.

Still this volume is limited by a self-imposed time constraint. We intended to publish something as soon as feasible regarding the papal message. Hence potential authors were asked to respond within four months of receiving their invitation, and this precluded many from being able to contribute an essay for this volume. Still we believe that the volume is representative and that the opinions here expressed, both measured and approving, are invaluable for the broader discussion of the issues raised by John Paul II. We also see this as just the beginning of a new and creative engagement of the Church and the Academy.

As a conclusion to this Preface and with the expectation that it will be of some help to the reader, I would like to present a brief summary of the papal message and of the responses of our contributors.

Summary of the Papal Message

1. General movement towards openness, dialogue, and interdependence.

The Pope cites the Christian ecumenical movement and the inter-religious dialogue among world religions as signs of openess. He also points to the move towards unification in the sciences, specifically in physics and biology.

2. What unity does and does not mean.

According to the Pope, unity means an integration of diversity, bringing greater fulfillment for each dialogue partner. Still unity is not synthesis or simple identity. It is not the creation of a new discipline but the search for a "common ground" which respects the limitations and competencies of each discipline. It is of crucial importance that each side possess its own foundations, procedures, interpretations, and conclusions. Neither can be the necessary premise for the other.

3. How can we obtain unity?

Rather than appealing to an *ad hoc* strategy to introduce scientific discoveries within the horizon of the Church, the Pope locates the process of obtaining unity squarely within theological method proper. This method, being faith seeking understanding, requires that one incorporates proven scientific and philosophical theories for theological purposes and for the illumination of Christian beliefs.

The Pope adds two precautions at the outset. First, the Church must restrict itself to only those scientific and philosophical theories which are well supported. Second, the Church should not seek to adjudicate the truth of the findings from science or philosophy. Finally he challenges contemporary theologians to do as well in this era, and with today's philosophy, as was done in the medieval period.

4. Who benefits and why?

The Pope argues that both sides can benefit from the exchange. The Church can benefit since it should help rid theology of error, superstition, and pseudo-science. Science also has the potential to benefit, since the dialogue might help science avoid absolutizing its methods or becoming an unconscious religion. In addition, dialogue provides both the Church and science an opportunity to make a greater contribution to the human community.

5. What do we need to get the vision underway?

The single most urgent need, according to the Pope, is for some theologians to be trained in science. Likewise the Church needs clergy-scientists to work at bridge ministries, facilitating the intellectual task of the science - faith dialogue while reflecting on moral issues raised by technology. Most of all the Church needs to engage in basic theological research which takes into view science and technology.

Summary of Responses

1. Many authors urge that we get beyond the old warfare mentality that existed to a certain degree between science and religion (Blackwell, Dulles, Ruether). Regge expresses a concern frequently raised, that the Church now settle the issue of Galileo's condemnation. Fortunately this concern has been, at least in part, met by Pope John Paul II's statement on Galileo in 1984.

2. Several authors emphasize the variety of ways in which the relationship between science and theology has been described, including the similarities and differences between science and religion (Dulles, Rolston, Townes). In the process, as Blackwell and others pointed out, it is crucial for theologians to learn science.

3. Some called for a new epistemology to promote the dialogue. Kalenga argues for an epistemology based on the relation of opposites in Niels Bohr's interpretation of quantum mechanics. Townes and Dulles emphasize the role of faith in both fields. Others focus on theological method. Murphy calls for theologians to appropriate current discussions in the philosophy of science which show that theology can be seen as a science.

4. Several authors write on the kinds of conceptual changes one can expect if theology took science on board (Cobb, Johnson, Torrance). Pannenberg emphasizes the role of philosophy in bridging theology and science, while Cobb gives a critique of dualist philosophy based on outmoded science. Mitcham argues that other views besides critical realism be pursued, while Fang describes some of the positive effects theology has had on the historical and contemporary development of science. McMullin emphasizes the provisional character of science, noting the effect this could have on theologies which appropriate science. He highlighted the remarks by the Pope on the Aristotelian hylomorphism where John Paul insists that the Church should not try to determine the truth in domains other than theology.

5. A number of writers attempt to suggest how the dialogue might go in both directions, effecting theology, philosophy , *and* science. This includes a sharp ethical critique of science (Cobb, Ellis, Mitcham, Regge, Ruether) and a concern for ecology (Johnson).

6. Several authors stress the need to turn the focus to biological issues (Eaves, Pannenberg, Rolston, Schmitz-Moorman) as well as other areas in physics, such as chaos theory (Johnson).

7. Finally Blackwell and Schmitz-Moorman stress the need for serious institutional support for the dialogue.

It has been a pleasure for me to edit this book with George Coyne and Bill Stoeger. I would also like to thank the contributors all of whom so graciously responded to demanding schedules.

Robert John Russell
Center for Theology and the Natural Sciences
Berkeley, California
June 1990

---

1. *Origins, NC Documentary Service* 16 (1986) 122; see also *Galileo Galilei: Toward a Resolution of 350 Years of Debate, 1633-1983*, ed. Cardinal Paul Poupard (Pittsburgh: Duquesne University Press, 1987) and *The Galileo Affair: A Meeting of Faith and Science*, eds. G. V. Coyne, M. Heller, and J. Zycinski (Vatican: Specola Vaticana, 1985).

2. *Physics, Philosophy, and Theology: A Common Quest for Understanding*, eds. R. J. Russell, W.R. Stoeger, and G.V. Coyne
(Notre Dame:IN; University of Notre Dame Press, 1988).

**MESSAGE OF HIS HOLINESS
POPE JOHN PAUL II**

To the Reverend George V. Coyne, S.J.
Director of the Vatican Observatory

"Grace to you and peace from God our Father and the Lord Jesus Christ" (Eph 1:2).

As you prepare to publish the papers presented at the Study Week held at Castelgandolfo on 21–26 September 1987, I take the occasion to express my gratitude to you and through you to all who contributed to that important initiative. I am confident that the publication of these papers will ensure that the fruits of that endeavour will be further enriched.

The three hundredth anniversary of the publication of Newton's <u>Philosophiae Naturalis Principia Mathematica</u> provided an appropriate occasion for the Holy See to sponsor a Study Week that investigated the multiple relationships among theology, philosophy and the natural sciences. The man so honoured, Sir Isaac Newton, had himself devoted much of his life to these same issues, and his reflections upon them can be found throughout his major works, his unfinished manuscripts and his vast correspondence. The publication of your own papers from this Study Week, taking up again some of the same questions which this great genius explored, affords me the opportunity to thank you for the efforts you devoted to a subject of such paramount importance. The theme of your conference, "Our Knowledge of God and Nature: Physics, Philosophy and Theology", is assuredly a crucial one for the contemporary world. Because of its importance, I should like to address some issues which the interactions among natural science, philosophy, and theology present to the Church and to human society in general.

The Church and the Academy engage one another as two very different but major institutions within human civilization and world culture. We bear before God enormous responsibilities for the human condition because historically we have had and continue to have a major influence on the development of ideas and values and on the course of human action. We both have histories stretching back over thousands of years: the learned, academic community dating back to the origins of culture, to the city and the library and the school, and the Church with her historical roots in ancient Israel. We have come into contact often during these centuries, sometimes in mutual support, at other times in those needless conflicts which have marred both our histories. In your conference we met again, and it was altogether fitting that as we approach the close of this millennium we initiated a series of reflections together upon the world as we touch it and as it shapes and challenges our actions.

So much of our world seems to be in fragments, in disjointed pieces. So much of human life is passed in isolation or in hostility. The division between rich nations and poor nations continues to grow; the contrast between northern and southern regions of our planet becomes ever more marked and intolerable. The antagonism between races and religions splits countries into warring camps; historical animosities show no signs of abating. Even within the academic community, the separation between truth and values persists, and the isolation of their several cultures – scientific, humanistic and religious – makes common discourse difficult if not at times impossible.

But at the same time we see in large sectors of the human community a growing critical openness towards people of different cultures and backgrounds, different competencies and viewpoints. More and more frequently, people are seeking intellectual coherence and collaboration, and are discovering values and experiences they have in common even within their diversities. This openness, this dynamic interchange, is a notable feature of the international scientific communities themselves, and is based on common interests, common goals and a common enterprise, along with a deep awareness that the insights and attainments of one are often important for the progress of the other. In a similar but more subtle way this has occurred and is continuing to occur among more diverse groups – among the communities that make up the Church, and even between the scientific community and the Church herself. This drive is essentially a movement towards the kind of unity which resists homogenization and relishes diversity. Such community is determined by a common meaning and by a shared understanding that evokes a sense of mutual involvement. Two groups which may seem initially to have nothing in common can begin to enter into community with one another by discovering a common goal, and this in turn can lead to broader areas of shared understanding and concern.

As never before in her history, the Church has entered into the movement for the union of all Christians, fostering common study, prayer, and discussions that "all may be one" (Jn 17:20). She has attempted to rid herself of every vestige of anti–semitism and to emphasize her origins in and her religious debt to Judaism. In reflection and prayer, she has reached out to the great world religions, recognizing the values we all hold in common and our universal and utter dependence upon God.

Within the Church herself, there is a growing sense of "world–church", so much in evidence at the last Ecumenical Council in which bishops native to every continent – no longer predominantly of European or even Western origin – assumed for the first time their common responsibility for the entire Church. The documents from that Council and of the magisterium have reflected this new world–consciousness both in their content and in their attempt to address all people of good will. During this century, we have witnessed a dynamic tendency to reconciliation and unity that has taken many forms within the Church.

Nor should such a development be surprising. The Christian community in moving so emphatically in this direction is realizing in greater intensity the activity of Christ within her: "For God was in Christ, reconciling the world to himself" (2 Cor 5:19). We ourselves are called to be a continuation of this reconciliation of human beings, one with another and all with God. Our very nature as Church entails this commitment to unity.

Turning to the relationship between religion and science, there has been a definite, though still fragile and provisional, movement towards a new and more nuanced interchange. We have begun to talk to one another on deeper levels than before, and with greater openness towards one another's perspectives. We have begun to search together for a more thorough understanding of one another's disciplines, with their competencies and their limitations, and especially for areas of common ground. In doing so we have uncovered important questions which concern both of us, and which are vital to the larger human community we both serve. It is crucial that this common search based on critical openness and interchange should not only continue but also grow and deepen in its quality and scope.

For the impact each has, and will continue to have, on the course of civilization and on the world itself, cannot be overestimated, and there is so much that each can offer the other. There is, of course, the vision of the unity of all things and all peoples in Christ, who is active and present with us in our daily lives – in our struggles, our sufferings, our joys and in our searchings – and who is the focus of the Church's life and witness. This vision carries with it into the larger community a deep reverence for all that is, a hope and assurance that the fragile goodness, beauty and life we see in the universe is moving towards a completion and fulfilment which will not be overwhelmed by the forces of dissolution and death. This vision also provides a strong support for the values which are emerging both from our knowledge and appreciation of creation and of ourselves as the products, knowers and stewards of creation.

The scientific disciplines too, as is obvious, are endowing us with an understanding and appreciation of our universe as a whole and of the incredibly rich variety of intricately related processes and structures which constitute its animate and inanimate components. This knowledge has given us a more thorough understanding of ourselves and of our humble yet unique role within creation. Through technology it also has given us the capacity to travel, to communicate, to build, to cure, and to probe in ways which would have been almost unimaginable to our ancestors. Such knowledge and power, as we have discovered, can be used greatly to enhance and improve our lives or they can be exploited to diminish and destroy human life and the environment even on a global scale.

The unity we perceive in creation on the basis of our faith in Jesus Christ as Lord of the universe, and the correlative unity for which we strive in our human communities, seems to be reflected and even reinforced in what contemporary science is revealing to us. As we behold the incredible development of scientific research we detect an underlying movement towards the discovery of levels of law and process which unify created reality and which at the same time have given rise to the vast diversity of structures and organisms which constitute the physical and biological, and even the psychological and sociological, worlds.

Contemporary physics furnishes a striking example. The quest for the unification of all four fundamental physical forces – gravitation, electro–magnetism, the strong and weak nuclear interactions – has met with increasing success. This unification may well combine discoveries from the sub–atomic and the cosmological domains and shed light both on the origin of the universe and, eventually, on the origin of the laws and constants which govern its evolution. Physicists possess a detailed though incomplete and provisional knowledge of elementary particles and of the fundamental forces through which they interact at low and intermediate energies. They now have an acceptable theory unifying the electro–magnetic and weak nuclear forces, along with much less adequate but still promising grand unified field theories which attempt to incorporate the strong nuclear interaction as well. Further in the line of this same development, there are already several detailed suggestions for the final stage, superunification, that is, the unification of all four fundamental forces, including gravity. Is it not important for us to note that in a world of such detailed specialization as contemporary physics there exists this drive towards convergence?

In the life sciences, too, something similar has happened. Molecular biologists have probed the structure of living material, its functions and its processes of replication. They have discovered that the same underlying constituents serve in the make–up of all living organisms on earth and constitute both the genes and the proteins which these genes code. This is another impressive manifestation of the unity of nature.

By encouraging openness between the Church and the scientific communities, we are not envisioning a disciplinary unity between theology and science like that which exists within a given scientific field or within theology proper. As dialogue and common searching continue, there will be growth towards mutual understanding and a gradual uncovering of common concerns which will provide the basis for further research and discussion. Exactly what form that will take must be left to the future. What is important, as we have already stressed, is that the dialogue should continue and grow in depth and scope. In the process we must overcome every regressive tendency to a unilateral reductionism, to fear, and to self–imposed isolation. What is critically important is that each discipline should continue to enrich, nourish and challenge the other to be more fully what it can be and to contribute to our vision of who we are and who we are becoming.

We might ask whether or not we are ready for this crucial endeavour. Is the community of world religions, including the Church, ready to enter into a more thorough–going dialogue with the scientific community, a dialogue in which the integrity of both religion and science is supported and the advance of each is fostered? Is the scientific community now prepared to open itself to Christianity, and indeed to all the great world religions, working with us all to build a culture that is more humane and in that way more divine? Do we dare to risk the honesty and the courage that this task demands? We must ask ourselves whether both science and religion will contribute to the integration of human culture or to its fragmentation. It is a single choice and it confronts us all.

For a simple neutrality is no longer acceptable. If they are to grow and mature, peoples cannot continue to live in separate compartments, pursing totally divergent interests from which they evaluate and judge their world. A divided community fosters a fragmented vision of the world; a community of interchange encourages its members to expand their partial perspectives and form a new unified vision.

Yet the unity that we seek, as we have already stressed, is not identity. The Church does not propose that science should become religion or religion science. On the contrary, unity always presupposes the diversity and the integrity of its elements. Each of these members should become not less itself but more itself in a dynamic interchange, for a unity in which one of the elements is reduced to the other is destructive, false in its promises of harmony, and ruinous of the integrity of its components. We are asked to become one. We are not asked to become each other.

To be more specific, both religion and science must preserve their autonomy and their distinctiveness. Religion is not founded on science nor is science an extension of religion. Each should possess its own principles, its pattern of procedures, its diversities of interpretation and its own conclusions. Christianity possesses the source of its justification within itself and does not expect science to constitute its primary apologetic. Science must bear witness to its own worth. While each can and should support the other as distinct dimensions of a common human culture, neither ought to assume that it forms a necessary premise for the other. The unprecedented opportunity we have today is for a common interactive relationship in which each discipline retains its integrity and yet is radically open to the discoveries and insights of the other.

But why is critical openness and mutual interchange a value for both of us? Unity involves the drive of the human mind towards understanding and the desire of the human spirit for love. When human beings seek to understand the multiplicities that surround them, when they seek to make sense of experience, they do so by bringing many factors into a common vision. Understanding is achieved when many data are unified by a common structure. The one illuminates the many; it makes sense of the whole. Simple multiplicity is chaos; an insight, a single model, can give that chaos structure and draw it into intelligibility. We move towards unity as we move towards meaning in our lives. Unity is also the consequence of love. If love is genuine, it moves not towards the assimilation of the other but towards union with the other. Human community begins in desire when that union has not been achieved, and it is completed in joy when those who have been apart are now united.

In the Church's earliest documents, the realization of community, in the radical sense of that word, was seen as the promise and goal of the Gospel: "That which we have seen and heard we proclaim also to you, so that you may have fellowship with us; and our fellowship is with the Father and with his Son Jesus Christ. And we are writing this that our joy may be complete" (1 Jn 1:3–3). Later the Church reached out to the sciences and to the arts, founding great universities and building momuments of surpassing beauty so that all things might be recapitulated in Christ (cf. Eph 1:10).

What, then, does the Church encourage in this relational unity between science and religion? First and foremost that they should come to understand one another. For too long a time they have been at arm's length. Theology has been defined as an effort of faith to achieve understanding, as <u>fides quaerens intellectum</u>. As such, it must be in vital interchange today with science just as it always has been with philosophy and other forms of learning. Theology will have to call on the findings of science to one degree or another as it pursues its primary concern for the human person, the reaches of freedom, the possibilities of Christian community, the nature of belief and the intelligibility of nature and history. The vitality and significance of theology for humanity will in a profound way be reflected in its ability to incorporate these findings.

Now this is a point of delicate importance, and it has to be carefully qualified. Theology is not to incorporate indifferently each new philosophical or scientific theory. As these findings become part of the intellectual culture of the time, however, theologians must understand them and test their value in bringing out from Christian belief some of the possibilities which have not yet been realized. The hylomorphism of Aristotelian natural philosophy, for example, was adopted by the medieval theologians to help them explore the nature of the sacraments and the hypostatic union. This did not mean that the Church adjudicated the truth or falsity of the Aristotelian insight, since that is not her concern. It did mean that this was one of the rich insights offered by Greek culture, that it needed to be understood and taken seriously and tested for its value in illuminating various areas of theology. Theologians might well ask, with respect to contemporary science, philosophy and the other areas of human knowing, if they have accomplished this extraordinarily difficult process as well as did these medieval masters.

If the cosmologies of the ancient Near Eastern world could be purified and assimilated into the first chapters of Genesis, might contemporary cosmology have something to offer to our reflections upon creation? Does an evolutionary perspective bring any light to bear upon theological anthropology, the meaning of the human person as the imago Dei, the problem of Christology -- and even upon the development of doctrine itself? What, if any, are the eschatological implications of contemporary cosmology, especially in light of the vast future of our universe? Can theological method fruitfully appropriate insights from scientific methodology and the philosophy of science?

Questions of this kind can be suggested in abundance. Pursuing them further would require the sort of intense dialogue with contemporary science that has, on the whole, been lacking among those engaged in theological research and teaching. It would entail that some theologians, at least, should be sufficiently well-versed in the sciences to make authentic and creative use of the resources that the best-established theories may offer them. Such an expertise would prevent them from making uncritical and overhasty use for apologetic purposes of such recent theories as that of the "Big Bang" in cosmology. Yet it would equally keep them from discounting altogether the potential relevance of such theories to the deepening of understanding in traditional areas of theological inquiry.

In this process of mutual learning, those members of the Church who are themselves either active scientists or, in some special cases, both scientists and theologians could serve as a key resource. They can also provide a much-needed ministry to others struggling to integrate the worlds of science and religion in their own intellectual and spiritual lives, as well as to those who face difficult moral decisions in matters of technological research and application. Such bridging ministries must be nurtured and encouraged. The Church long ago recognized the importance of such links by establishing the Pontifical Academy of Sciences, in which some of the world's leading scientists meet together regularly to discuss their researches and to convey to the larger community where the directions of discovery are tending. But much more is needed.

The matter is urgent. Contemporary developments in science challenge theology far more deeply than did the introduction of Aristotle into Western Europe in the thirteenth century. Yet these developments also offer to theology a potentially important resource. Just as Aristotelian philosophy, through the ministry of such great scholars as St Thomas Aquinas, ultimately came to shape some of the most profound expressions of theological doctrine, so can we not hope that the sciences of today, along with all forms of human knowing, may invigorate and inform those parts of the theological enterprise that bear on the relation of nature, humanity and God?

Can science also benefit from this interchange? It would seem that it should. For science develops best when its concepts and conclusions are integrated into the broader human culture and its concerns for ultimate meaning and value. Scientists cannot, therefore, hold themselves entirely aloof from the sorts of issues dealt with by philosophers and theologians. By devoting to these issues something of the energy and care they give to their research in science, they can help others realize more fully the human potentialities of their discoveries. They can also come to appreciate for themselves that these discoveries cannot be a genuine substitute for knowledge of the truly ultimate. Science can purify religion from error and superstition; religion can purify science from idolatry and false absolutes. Each can draw the other into a wider world, a world in which both can flourish.

For the truth of the matter is that the Church and the scientific community will inevitably interact; their options do not include isolation. Christians will inevitably assimilate the prevailing ideas about the world, and today these are deeply shaped by science. The only question is whether they will do this critically or unreflectively, with depth and nuance or with a shallowness that debases the Gospel and leaves us ashamed before history. Scientists, like all human beings, will make decisions upon what ultimately gives meaning and value to their lives and to their work. This they will do well or poorly, with the reflective depth that theological wisdom can help them attain, or with an unconsidered absolutizing of their results beyond their reasonable and proper limits.

Both the Church and the scientific community are faced with such inescapable alternatives. We shall make our choices much better if we live in a collaborative interaction in which we are called continually to be more. Only a dynamic relationship between theology and science can reveal those limits which support the integrity of either discipline, so that theology does not profess a pseudo–science and science does not become an unconscious theology. Our knowledge of each other can lead us to be more authentically ourselves. No one can read the history of the past century and not realize that crisis is upon us both. The uses of science have on more than one occasion proven massively destructive, and the reflections on religion have too often been sterile. We need each other to be what we must be, what we are called to be.

And so on this occasion of the Newton Tricentennial, the Church speaking through my ministry calls upon herself and the scientific community to intensify their constructive relations of interchange through unity. You are called to learn from one another, to renew the context in which science is done and to nourish the inculturation which vital theology demands. Each of you has everything to gain from such an interaction, and the human community which we both serve has a right to demand it from us.

Upon all who participated in the Study Week sponsored by the Holy See and upon all who will read and study the papers herein published I invoke wisdom and peace in our Lord Jesus Christ and cordially impart my Apostolic Blessing.

From the Vatican, 1 June, 1988

Joannes Paulus PP II

SCIENCE AND RELIGION: THE PAPAL CALL FOR AN OPEN DIALOGUE

Richard J. Blackwell

If Pope John Paul II's letter of 1 June 1988 on the relationship of science and religion receives the attention and implementation which it deserves from Catholic intellectuals and Church leaders, it may well mark the first step in a significantly new direction for Catholic culture. The letter is quite accurate and particularly clear in its diagnosis of the present state of the relation between science and religion. Its suggested remedy is both unusually bold and refreshingly free of the intellectual defensiveness which has characterized so many Church statements on science since the Counter Reformation. But although its challenge is strong, the letter is largely silent on issues of implementation and prognosis, particularly in regard to the bothersome question of whether the present condition of Catholic intellectual and ecclesiastical culture will tend to help or hinder the realization of the Pope's recommendations.

The letter's diagnosis is insightful and not subject to much disagreement. Unless the Church intends to abandon its interests in the First World, an unthinkable suggestion, it must come to a better understanding of, and interaction with, modern science and technology, which for some time now have been the dominant forces in Western culture. As the Pope says, isolation is not an option: ". . .the Church and the scientific community will inevitably interact" (M13). Moreover the timing for this is presently quite propitious. Both physics and the life sciences have clearly moved toward greater internal unification in the second half of this century. There are good reasons to believe that something similar may now also be underway in the human sciences, especially in psychology and in the neurobiology of thought processes. This thrust toward greater unity is prominent within the sciences.

However, the dialogue between religion and science has generally not been an exchange between equals. In the seventeenth century when this communication became urgent, the religious world enjoyed a cultural dominance over the newly born modern science of that day, a dominance which unfortunately resulted in the alienation of science from religion, especially as a consequence of the Galileo affair. After three centuries of stalemate the roles are now reversed; the combination of science and technology is now the dominant cultural force in the Western world and the interests of religion are at a disadvantage. In such cases of dialogue between unequals the dominant side is always tempted to claim to have all the answers or to have a universal method to that end. This is a fatal obstacle for communication.

As a result dialogue between science and religion in the past has often failed because it occurred so frequently in an atmosphere of mutual suspicion, if not hostility. However, as the Pope points out, the present thrust of the major components of modern science is toward a nonreductionistic integration within science in which the diverse sciences are preserved and enriched in the unity. This provides a model for a similar, more equal, and much more fruitful interaction between science and religion. The Pope's diagnosis is to be especially commended for its recognition of this promising new model for communication between science and religion.

The remedy prescribed is to work toward establishing precisely such a nonreductionistic and dynamic interaction between science and religion which would preserve and enhance the integrity of both fields. In this process each will unavoidably be changed by the other, if there is a genuine interaction. The boldness and nondefensiveness of the Pope's advice consist in part in this willingness to enter into a real intellectual exchange with science which will produce inevitable but specifically unpredictable reconceptualizations not only of science but also of religion. If this can be taken at full face value, the letter is a declaration of the end of the Counter Reformation mentality toward science in the Church – a much needed and long overdue development.

The Pope is quite explicit about this remedy. Just as the late medievals took the best science available to them, i.e., Aristotelian science, and used it as a tool to bring out the fuller meaning of religious beliefs, the Pope challenges modern theologians not to isolate themselves from the best in modern science, but instead to use it in the same way to formulate an integration (as defined above) with modern science and to develop an understanding of the Church's religious doctrines which will speak to the contemporary scientific world. This call for a creative paradigm shift, analogous to the Augustinian and Thomistic revolutions in medieval theology, is truly extraordinary. Can Catholic intellectuals meet this challenge? Will they be free to do so?

What is asked for is an enormous undertaking. For one thing the role of Thomism in the Church's thinking will need to be critically re-examined. As we see it, although the Thomistic synthesis has served the Church well, especially in the various branches of theology, it is ill suited to speak to the contemporary scientific culture and to account for modern science, which it predated by several centuries. New times call for a new synthesis. In our judgment, if St. Thomas were somehow reincarnated in our day, he would attempt to do now what he did then, i.e., to formulate a viable synthesis of Catholic religious beliefs with contemporary science.

This call for a new conceptual synthesis is, of course, not explicitly stated in the Pope's letter, but seems to us to be a reasonable inference from it. But even if that inference is not intended, we would argue nonetheless that such a new synthesis is required for a fruitful interaction between science and religion. The reason is that Thomism is inextricably interwoven with the same Aristotelian science which was repudiated by the founders of modern science in the seventeenth century. Continued allegiance to that science blocks communication with modern science. Can Thomism be freed from those features of its Aristotelian heritage which are inimical to science after Darwin (e.g., the immutability of forms) without fatally undercutting itself in the process?

Granting this reading of the letter, the very boldness and enormous scope of the Pope's remedy casts some shadows on the prognosis for its successful implementation. First one cannot simply put in an order for creative thinking as though one were ordering a new auto or a new building. However creative thinking occurs (and we know rather little about this), it is agreed that it is not a case of simply following a fixed set of production rules. The most that can be done is to try to establish conditions which are favorable for creative intellectual work, and hope that this fertile ground will produce results in time, although there can be no guarantee of success. In this regard Catholic culture is presently very weak. For a long time science education in the training of Catholic clergy, and thereby of most Catholic theologians, has been minimal at best. This is one of the main reasons why so little progress has been made to date on relating science and religion.

The situation is not much better at the large number of Catholic colleges and universities in the United States. Although a great deal of scientific education, and to a lesser extent scientific research, occurs at these institutions, it is mostly directed toward professional and technical career preparation of the students with little interaction between the science faculties, philosophers, and theologians. What is sorely lacking is a group of scholars expertly trained in both science and philosophy and/or theology. Only a few individuals who are established experts on both sides of the dialogue are to be found in the Catholic world, usually isolated at different colleges and universities. At present the University of Notre Dame has the only advanced graduate program in the history and philosophy of science among Catholic universities in the United States. Catholic scholars are few and far between at national meetings of the History of Science Society and the Philosophy of Science Association.

With such a paucity of Catholic scholars and programs focused on the science-religion issue in this country, the Catholic intellectual environment is not likely to produce the interaction recommended by the Pope. A redirection of priorities and programs will be needed before an implementation of the Pope's letter can be said to be realistic.

The matter is complicated by another factor which is probably more of an obstacle. As mentioned earlier, if the recommended interaction between science and religion actually occurs in any substantive way, both sides in the exchange will be significantly affected in ways that cannot be specifically determined ahead of time. Is the Church ready to take this risk? This dialogue is a two-way street, and travelers will return changed from the experience. Another way of putting this is that there undoubtedly will be many false starts and dead ends as scholars try to creatively rethink the relations between science and religion. Will the guardians of orthodoxy in the Church allow this to happen, indeed even encourage it, to attain the Pope's goals, or will they take the easier and safer course of invoking condemnation on what is novel?

The Church's history in this area, including even more recent years, has not been encouraging. In short the interaction called for between science and religion requires a uncustomary degree of freedom of thought in Catholic intellectual culture which will be difficult to establish and to maintain. How widely shared is the Pope's plea for interaction at the other levels of the Church's organization where such key decisions on orthodoxy are often made? Also, since this would be a long term project, will future Popes endorse and implement the present Pope's letter?

In summary, our reflections on the letter have generated our enthusiastic agreement on its diagnosis and suggested remedy for the science-religion relationship. The Church should not and cannot continue to neglect its relation to science if it hopes to have the good news of the revelation heard and understood in the scientific culture of the contemporary Western world. Over the centuries the Church has repeatedly adapted its message to new and different cultures; it is being called upon to do so again; and this in turn will not be the final version of the Church's relation to the world, since scientific culture itself continually changes in time. The Pope's challenge is to call our attention to this fact and to this need.

On the other hand we are far less sanguine about the possibilities for meeting this challenge. Catholic intellectual life on both sides of the science-religion dialogue is at present poorly prepared for the task. We need to improve on the vigor, energy, and freedom of the Catholic cultural environment as a first step. The *sine qua non* to implement the suggestions in the Pope's letter is a significant rebirth of Catholic intellectual life in the sciences, in philosophy, and in theology, a rebirth which will encourage creative minds to interrelate these areas in new ways at the foundational level in an atmosphere of academic freedom. This will be a risky undertaking for the Church. But to do nothing is even more of a risk.

ONE STEP FURTHER

John B. Cobb, Jr

I respond to Pope John Paul II's message with deep gratitude. I am a part of the religious community, and, although I am not a Roman Catholic, I recognize that on many matters the Pope speaks for this whole community, even beyond the Christian one, as does no one else. Accordingly, I feel particular satisfaction when, as in this case, he fulfills his extraordinary responsibility with such sensitivity and insight as are here expressed. I know of no finer statement on the subject of theology and the natural sciences.

Therefore, if I thought critical comment from those for whom he has spoken would in any way detract from the authority of his statement, I would be silent. But I find a second point for which to be grateful. The statement comes with an invitation for critical response. It is presented not as the final word on the issue but as a basis for conversation that can carry still further our shared understanding of a matter of great urgency. To offer a written response, therefore, seems a better expression of appreciation than silence.

I experience my own criticism not as a rejection of anything that is said but as expressing a need to push for more. The statement calls, movingly and convincingly, for a unity in which diversity remains. I want to emphasize, more than is clearly done in the statement, that neither the scientific communities nor the Church, neither science nor theology, can remain internally unaffected by the quest for unity.

For the Pope to make a statement about the need for change within the scientific community and within science itself could be dangerous. He is probably wise to emphasize the autonomy of scientific communities and of the sciences in view of the deep-seated suspicion among scientists that the Church wants to restrict their freedom or impose theological dogma on their findings. But someday, we may hope, these suspicions can fade, and even the Pope will be able to speak bluntly without fear of being misinterpreted. Meanwhile, those of us who possess no political or ecclesiastical power may be the best ones to press the issue.

When we speak of the scientific community, we need to recognize how very much it is tied today to research for military and other nationalistic purposes. The vision of scientists as operating out of pure love of truth has still its element of verisimilitude, but as a sociological judgment about the scientific community as a whole it falsifies more than it reveals. Funding sources largely determine what is investigated, and when these do not reflect national competition for power, they generally reflect the interests of those who have the wealth to employ scientific talent. Very little research is really for the sake of those for whom the Church cares the most: the powerless and the oppressed.

Furthermore, even when research is guided in part by the needs of the poor, as for example in the Green Revolution, projects are conceived paternalistically and with tunnel vision. The poor are rarely involved by scientists in determining their own needs, and in the process of meeting one need the situation is often worsened in other ways. For research scientists to say that this is not their affair, that their discoveries are morally neutral and can be used for good or ill, only shows how deep-seated is the problem. Resources for scientific research are limited. The scientific community does participate in deciding how these resources are used. There are impressive instances of scientists acting with great responsibility, as when large numbers in the United States refused to participate in SDI research. But this was a remarkable exception to the general rule that their research is directed by the availability of funding. The scientific community as a whole does little to insure that research serves the common good. As a result, most of it does not. As scientific communities and the Church move toward unity, this will change.

In addition to political reasons for papal silence on this matter, there is another, substantive one. Despite the title, the message deals more with science and theology than with the relations of the two communities. Attention is focused on the contributions of scientists to the shaping of a new world view in its relation to what Christians believe about the world. When issues are dealt with in this way, the sociological and ethical concerns I have noted fade to the background. Any claim that science as such will be changed through unity with theology appears, at first glance, wrong. Surely scientific theory is an expression of the quest for truth which Christians can only admire!

Even here, however, I demur. The Pope's statement could suggest a kind of laissez-faire that I do not support. Of course, I do not mean in any simplistic way that Christians should ask scientists to introduce Christological ideas into their physics. That would be absurd. But I do mean that when physics is studied historically we find that its basic conceptuality does not arise simply out of empirical evidence but also out of habits of language and belief that are subject to philosophical criticism. Physicists are not necessarily the best critics of their own assumptions, models, and presuppositions, since their training and socialization channel their energies elsewhere. Philosophers once supposed that criticism of such assumptions was part of their task, but the compartmentalization of scholarship has discouraged this. The implications of the Pope's general vision of an interconnected world lead toward ending this compartmentalization of knowledge and encouraging mutual criticism and support between philosophers and scientists. I am only asking that this be made more explicit and that its importance be stressed.

I have spoken above of philosophers rather than theologians, but on this point I am in full agreement with the Pope. He makes it clear that there can be no wall between these two groups, as some of my Protestant colleagues like to think. Theologians cannot be neutral among philosophies; hence they cannot be neutral with respect to the philosophical assumptions on the basis of which various sciences have developed. For example, they cannot be content that some sciences have adopted mutually incompatible assumptions. The drive for the unity of science, currently weak in most of the scientific communities, needs the impetus of encouragement from theology. It can only be successful through considerable reform in the sciences themselves.

Thus far, I have been asking for a clearer statement of the need for and means of a movement toward unity which can and should transform science and the scientific communities. I turn now to the impact of this movement on the Church and on theology. Less is required here, since the Pope himself has indicated how theology needs to be affected by science. He rightly warns against too close a tie to the most recent theory, any suggestion that theology depends primarily on science, and also any notion that theology should remain unchanged by scientific advances. I applaud his formulations.

Even so, I would emphasize still more strongly the intimacy of the connections. Most people today, in and out of the Church, see the world in ways deeply influenced by the science of the recent past. Much of this is healthy. When we reflect on the role of superstition throughout Western history, and on its continuing power today, we can only hope that science will grow in influence as an ally of the Church in combating this.

But, of course, there remain questions about what is superstitious and what is not. Is the belief in the real presence of Christ in the sacraments a superstition? Many formulations of the doctrine may have had superstitious elements, but Christians are convinced that the doctrine as such is not superstitious. Yet according to some world views, closely bound up with assumptions influential in shaping some sciences, even the best formulated Christian doctrines are disqualified. This suggests that theologians, scientists, and philosophers need to work together both to modify the doctrine and to modify the world views that are in such sharp tension with it. Theologians cannot simply accept dominant world views from the sciences and adapt to them. On the other hand, they cannot live with the idea that one world view is true for science, another for theology.

Another example of needed change raises quite different issues. This has to do with the relation of human beings to other living things and especially to other sentient beings. Both the scientific communities and the Church have been overwhelmingly insensitive to the suffering we human beings impose in increasing measure on our fellow creatures, often for quite trivial purposes. This insensitivity is based on, or at least justified by, a dualism between human beings and everything else, a dualism that is not supported by either scientific evidence or the Bible. Its strongest support is in philosophies that are inadequate for both communities. Critical reconsideration of our views of the world should open us to the actual evidence of our immersion in the natural world and our kinship with other creatures and should reshape our practice to conform to what we know.

These are but two minor illustrations of the importance of a task on which far too little effort has been expended: the development of a world view that is at once Christian and scientific. Such a world view will necessarily be very different both from the one now dominant in science and from those that are expressed in most current theologies. Here and there individual scientists, philosophers, and theologians have made important contributions. Those who are personally both scientists and theologians have been particularly helpful, as the Pope has noted. But the task is enormous. The Church's stake, indeed, the world's stake, in advancing this enterprise is far greater than is generally realized. The work requires undergirding and support. It is hard to see any other ongoing source of such undergirding and support than the Roman Catholic Church.

For this reason, I rejoice that the Church held a Study Week to celebrate the tercentenary of Newton's *Philosophiae Naturalis Principia Mathematica*, that there is a Pontifical Academy of Sciences, that one of the Church's loyal sons has established a Center for Theology and the Natural Sciences, and that the Pope has spoken with wisdom and force about the need for unity. May the effort go beyond the exchange of ideas and mutual appreciation to a mutual transformation of two communities! May the Christian Church fulfill its calling to bring realistic meaning to a confused and fragmented world!

SCIENCE AND THEOLOGY

Avery Dulles, S.J.

Pope John Paul II's message occasioned by the Castel Gandolfo conference on Physics, Philosophy, and Theology deserves careful study.[1] One can hardly disagree with Ernan McMullin that "it is without a doubt the most important and most specific papal statement on the relations between religion and science in recent times."[2] The tone of the message is open, confident, and encouraging. Without preempting the prerogatives of working theologians, philosophers, and scientists to make their own applications, the Holy Father proposes a program that appears to be feasible, valuable, and even necessary for the good of all concerned.

The general position taken by John Paul II may be indicated by reference to the standard typology of the relationships between religion and the sciences: conflict, separation, fusion, dialogue, and the integration.[3]

Very clearly the Pope rejects the position of conflict, in which it would be necessary to choose either science or religion to the exclusion of the other. This rejection can take either of two forms. One form is a "scientism" such as that of Thomas Henry Huxley, who asserted in a lay sermon in 1866: "There is but one kind of knowledge, and but one method of acquiring it," namely science.[4] By the universal application of scientific method, positivists believed, it would be possible to dispel the dark clouds of dogma and inaugurate a bright new era of free assent to universally acknowledged truth. This triumphalist variety of scientism is not yet dead. The periodical *Free Inquiry*, for example, promotes science and reason as opposed to faith and religion.[5] The "scientific" program tends to reduce quality to quantity and to emphasize the technological aspects of life. But it also makes room for a certain mystical exaltation of science, to the point where it becomes a pseudo-religion, involving what the Pope in his message calls an "unconscious theology" (M14). Jacques Monod and Carl Sagan are sometimes cited, though not by the Pope, as examples of scientists who tend to extrapolate beyond the proper limits of their own discipline.

On the other hand, the Pope no less firmly rejects the alternative possibility – the religionism of those who oppose science in the name of faith. In this framework theology becomes, as the Pope warns, a pseudo-science (M14). This may be judged to have occurred in the case of the "creation science" taught by some American fundamentalists. The "creationist" position, as Gilkey and others have shown, is in fact anti-scientific.[6] According to the sounder view, held by the Pope in his message, faith cannot do the work of science, nor can the Bible function as a textbook of astronomy or biology.

The second major position that the Pope rejects may be called separationism. Some thoughtful Christians solve the problem by relegating religion and science to separate spheres. This kind of separation has become almost axiomatic in Protestant theology since Immanuel Kant, who confined the competence of theoretical reason to the order of phenomena, and regarded religious beliefs as deliverances of the practical intellect. Not only liberal theologians, such as Albrecht Ritschl and Adolf Harnack, but also Neo-Orthodox thinkers such as Karl Barth, Rudolf Bultmann, and Paul Tillich, accepted this division into two spheres. In our own day theologians influenced by Ludwig Wittgenstein frequently say, as does Richard Braithwaite, that religious language is not intended to communicate cognitive truth but to recommend a way of life and to evoke a set of attitudes. In a similar vein, George Lindbeck maintains that doctrinal statements are "communally authoritative rules of discourse, attitude, and action."[7] In all these theories the dogmas of the Church, even though they may seem to describe objective realities, are reinterpreted as symbolic expressions describing the inner experience of the speaker or regulating the conduct of the worshipping community. Science, by contrast, is held to be informative and to make claims about objective reality. A peace between religion and science is achieved in these systems, but only at the price of depriving religion of its claim to say anything true about the world of ordinary experience.

John Paul II refuses to settle for a world divided into two cultures, humanistic and scientific, as described by C. P. Snow in his classic essay.[8] Interaction, according to the Pope, is necessary for the proper functioning of both religion and science. Without it science can become destructive and religion sterile (M14).

For his program of unification the Pope gives several arguments. The human mind, in its quest for understanding, inevitably seeks to unify and synthesize. By unifying many data we are able to make sense of the whole (M9). Unity, likewise, is a demand of love. A fully inclusive human community is promoted to the extent that all the members are able to share, and profit from, one another's insights. Finally, the relational unity between science and religion is a demand of Christian faith, which sees all things as created in and for Christ (Col. 1:16-17) and as destined to be reconciled through him (Col. 1:20; Eph. 1:10). The Pope attributes the founding of universities by the Church to this faith-conviction (M10).

While repudiating separationism, which could be called a kind of methodological Nestorianism, John Paul II also rejects the opposite extreme of fusion, which might be compared with Monophysitism in Christology. Science, he warns, is not called to become theology nor is theology called to become science. Nor, finally, should both of them be swallowed up in some *tertium quid* that would be a higher integration of both. The Pope wants each discipline to retain its own principles and its own identity while challenging and being challenged by the other (M7). He does not envision a disciplinary unity between theology and science.

Positively, then, the Pope accepts a fourth position – that of dialogue and interaction. In this relationship neither science nor religion should either seek to dominate the other or submit uncritically to the deliverances of the other. Yet each discipline should profit from, and contribute to, the attainments of the other. In a memorable paragraph the Pope explains:

> To be more specific, both religion and science must preserve their autonomy and their distinctiveness. Religion is not founded on science nor is science an extension of religion . . . . While each can and should support the other as distinct dimensions of a common human culture, neither ought to assume that it forms a necessary premise for the other. The unprecedented opportunity we have today is for a common interactive relationship in which each discipline retains its integrity and yet is radically open to the discoveries and insights of the other. (M8-9)

To suggest what he has in mind John Paul II gives two historical examples. The early chapters of Genesis, he points out, borrow fruitfully from the cosmologies of the ancient Near East, which afforded concepts and images that, with the necessary purification, could well serve to communicate revealed truth. In the Middle Ages, theologians borrowed from ancient Greek philosophy a whole panoply of technical concepts such as form and matter, substance and accident. Although the Church made use of such concepts, and further refined them, in exploring the sacraments and the hypostatic union, "this did not mean that the Church adjudicated the truth or falsity of the Aristotelian insight, since that is not her concern. It did mean that this was one of the rich insights offered by Greek culture, that it needed to be understood and taken seriously and tested for its value in illuminating various areas of theology." (M11) This last statement has considerable theological importance, since Pope Pius XII has been understood as teaching that the Church did certify the truth of the principles of Aristotelian and scholastic metaphysics.[9]

Pope John Paul II then goes on to encourage contemporary theologians to appropriate insights from scientific methodology and from the philosophy of science. Without explicitly mentioning the particular system of Teilhard de Chardin, which some critics have judged to be deficient either on scientific or on theological grounds, the Pope seems to encourage the adventurous spirit that motivated the great French paleontologist.

The type of program suggested by the Pope is actually being pursued on a number of fronts. Several examples from the realm of cosmology may here be mentioned. Some are convinced that the "Big Bang" theory of cosmic origins provides a scientific confirmation of the Christian doctrine of creation – a view that the Pope mentions with the warning that "uncritical and overhasty use" should not be made of the "Big Bang" theory for apologetic purposes (M11-12).[10] Others ask whether the scientifically predicted "cold death" of the universe, through the operation of the laws of thermodynamics, has something to say to Christian eschatology. Then again, it may be asked whether the "anthropic principle," according to which the universe seems to have been "fine-tuned" from its origins to produce and support human life, gives new relevance to classical arguments from design. Some theologians, moreover, believe that the principle of indeterminacy in Werner Heisenberg's quantum physics can be helpful in overcoming the dilemmas of freedom and necessity and in showing how Providence can act without violating the established order of nature. A number of theologians, finally, hold that Niels Bohr's principles of complementarity, according to which light exhibits both wavelike and corpuscular characteristics, could suggest new ways of dealing with mystery and paradox in theology. Yves Congar, for instance, asks whether the Eastern and Western traditions in Trinitarian theology should be seen as irreducibly different but complementary articulations of a mystery too rich for any one conceptual system.[11]

It may be premature to give definitive answers to any of these questions. In the spirit of the Pope's letter we may say that it is proper for theologians to state whether, and under what conditions, they could accept or welcome the new scientific hypotheses, and to explore the ways in which such hypotheses can provide new imagery and vocabulary for speaking about traditional Christian doctrines. Theologians should, however, be on guard against a facile concordism that would link the doctrines of faith too closely with fragile scientific hypotheses. Conversely, scientists, while they should refrain from proposing their theories as deductions from doctrines of Christian faith, may allow their religious faith to suggest lines of scientific investigation that would not otherwise have occurred to them. Scientists who are also believers will be reluctant to accept scientific hypotheses, such as Jacques Monod's doctrine of "chance and necessity," as long as these hypotheses seem incompatible with Christian faith.[12] In this connection it may be pertinent to recall that Pope Pius XII in 1950 asserted that the theory of polygenism, in certain forms, was unacceptable "since it is no way apparent how such an opinion can be reconciled" with the biblical and ecclesiastical teachings about original sin.[13]

One of the areas of dialogue suggested by the Pope concerns methodology (M11). Since early modern times it has been customary to accept a sharp contrast between the methods of science and theology. Blaise Pascal put the matter very strongly:

> Authority alone can enlighten us in these [historical] matters. But such authority has its principal force in theology, because there it is inseparable from truth, and truth is unobtainable in any other way. Thus, to give complete certitude concerning matters most incomprehensible to reason, it is sufficient to show that they are found in the sacred books, and to demonstrate the uncertainty of things that seem quite evident, it is enough to point out that they are not contained in Scripture. For the principles of theology are above both nature and reason. Since the mind of man is too feeble to attain them by its own efforts, it cannot achieve such lofty understanding unless it is borne by an almighty and supernatural force.
>
> But in matters that lie within the scope of the senses and of reason, the situation is far different. Here authority is useless; reason alone is in a position to know them. The two types of knowledge have their separate prerogatives. In the former area authority has all the advantage; here reason reigns in its turn.[14]

Developments in twentieth-century science and theology have shown this contrast to be exaggerated. Science is not committed to reason alone nor faith to authority alone. Each discipline works with a subtle combination of faith and experience, intuition and reason, imagination and deduction, personal insight and communal wisdom.

The role of faith in science has been strongly emphasized by Max Planck, among others. In an interview he put the matter very dramatically: "Anybody who has been seriously engaged in scientific work of any kind realizes that over the gates of the temple of science are written the words: *Ye must have faith*. It is a quality which the scientist cannot dispense with."[15] Einstein, Eddington, Heisenberg, and Oppenheimer could easily be quoted to the same effect.[16] The scientist has to act on the premises that an external world exists, that it is orderly, and that the mind has the capacity to grasp the order that is there. Further acts of faith are demanded for anyone to become committed to the scientific enterprise, to learn the current state of the discipline, and to advance toward new discoveries. At each stage one must put one's own trust in some idea or principle that could conceivably be false – in other words, one must make an act of natural or scientific faith. Thus faith, in a broad and generic sense, may be seen as a bond between science and theology.

Conversely, religious faith depends to some extent upon reason. Revelation could not be made except to a rational being, for a brute animal could not grasp the meaning or credibility of God's word. Theology, as a methodical inquiry into the significance and coherence of the revealed message, is eminently a work of reason.

Another link between science and religion is the authority of tradition in each discipline. Admittedly, many scientists since the Enlightenment have been in some ways hostile to authority and tradition. As Michael Polanyi reminds us, the founders of the Royal Society took as their device *Nullius in Verba*.[17] But historians of science have clearly shown that tradition plays a role in science no less important than its role in theology. In his little book entitled *Tradition in Science*, Werner Heisenberg points out that the scientist relies heavily on tradition to supply the state of the question, the problems to be solved, and the concepts, paradigms and methods that may be helpful for the solution.[18] In science, as in theology, development occurs gradually. Progress would not be possible if past achievements were not remembered and employed.

Just as continuity has its place in science, so, conversely, change is a factor in religious knowledge. The theologian cannot be content simply to repeat the words of venerated predecessors. New problems must be addressed with new information and new methods of inquiry. In theology, as in the natural sciences, there can be sudden breakthroughs or "scientific revolutions" in which whole areas are perceived from a radically new perspective.[19]

Theologians, quite evidently, operate within a community of faith. They receive their faith from the Church, carry on their reflections within the Church, and offer the results of their labors to the Church for appraisal. Scientists, similarly, do not work in isolated independence. Polanyi makes the point that neophytes in the sciences must join the scientific community and submit to a process of formation in which they learn by example and supervised performance. He writes:

> This assimilation of great systems of articulate lore by
> novices of various grades is made possible only by a *previous
> act of affiliation*, by which the novice accepts apprenticeship to
> a community which cultivates this lore, appreciates its values
> and strives to act by its standards. This affiliation begins with

the fact that a child submits to education within a community, and is confirmed throughout life to the extent to which the adult continues to place exceptional confidence in the intellectual leaders of the same community.[20]

The scientific community is less formally organized than the Church. But it has, in its way, a hierarchy of leadership. Ecclesiastical officials control the transmission of Christian doctrine not only by direct teaching but also indirectly, by a variety of means such as the supervision of seminary appointments, ordinations, and theological publications. So, likewise, the leaders of the scientific community exercise a kind of doctrinal authority not only by their own utterances but also through their influence on the curriculum of instruction, the bestowal of honors and degrees, university appointments, fellowships, and the acceptance of articles for scholarly journals. The capacity "to grant or withhold opportunity for research, publication and teaching, to endorse or discredit contributions put forward by individuals" is, according to Polanyi, "indispensable for the continued existence of science." Without such controls the journals would be flooded with rubbish and valuable work would be banished to obscurity.[21]

These similarities, to be sure, are not identities. As John Paul II insists, science and theology do have distinct methods. Unlike religious faith, assent to scientific truth does not depend on divine grace. Science does not rest on an unalterable deposit of faith; it does not look back to unique, unrepeatable past events as its essential basis. Nor does the scientific community have a magisterium that claims to be divinely assisted and capable of rendering, on occasion, infallible judgments. Nevertheless the analogies are sufficient so that it may be possible, as the Pope suggests, for each to learn from the other.

The dialogue between faith and science can produce palpable benefits to both. For one thing, each discipline, by maintaining contact with the other, is protected from certain errors and excesses to which, by itself, it would be prone. On the one hand, theology is liberated from a naive or fundamentalistic reading of Scripture, such as that which played a part in the condemnation of Galileo,[22] and that which continues to thrive in "creation science." Through scientific education believers are able to overcome a superstitious or magical attitude that takes insufficient account of the established order of secondary causality. On the other hand, science is, as the Pope also remarks, purified "from idolatry and false absolutes" (M13). Pursued in isolation, the brilliant achievements of science can be destructive of higher values.

The mutual benefits flowing from dialogue are not only negative but also positive. This is apparent in the area of cosmology, on which the Pope is chiefly commenting. The theological imagination has been immensely enlarged by the fresh vistas offered by contemporary physics and astronomy. Theologians no longer discuss the doctrines of creation and providence in the narrow framework provided by ancient myths and philosophic systems. Creation means far more when understood in terms of the "infinite spaces" that made Pascal shudder with religious awe.[23] Providence and salvation history take on a wholly new significance when seen against the background of the billions of years of cosmic existence postulated by contemporary science but undreamt of by Bishop Ussher and his contemporaries.

Scientific cosmology, if enriched by the study of theological method, can gain a deeper realization of its own reliance on faith, tradition, community, and authority. Science can better understand its own nature and history by viewing its achievements in the light of religious thought. As the Pope remarks, science develops more successfully to the extent that "its concepts and conclusions are integrated into the broader human culture and its concerns for meaning and value" (M13). Insights of religious thinkers of the stature of Newman, Tillich, Teilhard de Chardin, and Rahner can help scientists to insert their findings into this broader framework and thus direct their labors to the well being of the human family.

Although the situation is still too fluid for solid syntheses to be achieved, the long warfare between sciences and theology may be coming to an end, and a new era of mutual friendship and collaboration may be at hand. The message of John Paul II, and the conference that occasioned that message, give substance to such hope.

Notes

1. The message of John Paul II will be cited in this article according to the norms of the editorial notes on the page of Contents.

2. Ernan McMullin, "Religious Book Week: Critics' Choices," *Commonweal* 116:5 (March 10, 1989) 149.

3. Many such typologies have been proposed; for example, that by Arthur R. Peacocke in his introduction to *The Sciences and Theology in the Twentieth Century*, edited by A. R. Peacocke (Notre Dame, IN: University of Notre Dame Press, 1981) xiii to xv. See also Ian G. Barbour, "Ways of Relating Science and Theology," in *Physics, Philosophy and Theology*: *A Common Quest for Understanding*, eds. R.J. Russell, W.R. Stoeger and G.V. Coyne (Notre Dame, IN: University of Notre Dame Press, 1988) 21-45. I am, in general, following Barbour's typology.

4. Quotation in Stanley L. Jaki, *The Relevance of Physics* (Chicago: University of Chicago Press, 1966) 499.

5. *Free Inquiry*, edited by Paul Kurtz, is published in Buffalo, NY, by the Council for Democratic and Secular Humanism.

6. Langdon Gilkey, *Creationism on Trial: Evolution and God at Little Rock* (San Francisco: Harper & Row, 1985).

7. George A. Lindbeck, *The Nature of Doctrine: Religion and Theology in a Postliberal Age* (Philadelphia: Westminster Press, 1984) 18.

8. C. P. Snow, *The Two Cultures and a Second Look* (Cambridge, Eng.: Cambridge University Press, 1965).

9. Pius XII, Encyclical *Humani generis* (*AAS* 42 [1950] 571); ET (New York: Paulist Press, 1950), nos. 48-49, pp. 14-15.

10. Pius XII in an address to the Pontifical Academic of Sciences in 1951 had maintained that modern science "has confirmed the contingency of the universe and also the well-founded deduction as to the epoch when the cosmos came forth from the hands of the Creator. Hence, creation took place in time: (*Catholic Mind* 50 [1952] 190). John Paul II has consistently been more reserved about the capacity of the physical sciences to establish or undermine the metaphysical and theological doctrine of creation. See John Paul II, "The Path of Scientific Discovery," *Origins* 11:18 (Oct. 15, 1981) 277-80. Stephen W. Hawking, in his *A Brief History of Time* (New York: Bantam Books, 1988) 116 and 141, hypothetically proposes a scientific theory according to which creation would have no beginning and thus no moment of creation.

11. Yves Congar, *Diversity and Communion* (Mystic, CT: Twenty-Third Publications, 1985) 74-76. Robert J. Russell, in his "Quantum Physics in Philosophical and Theological Perspective," in *Physics, Philosophy and Theology: A Common Quest for Understanding, op. cit.*, pp. 343-74, at pp. 359-61, gives a number of other attempted applications of the principle of complementarity in the realm of theology.

12. Cf. Jacques Monod, *Chance and Necessity* (New York, NY: A. Knopf, 1971); also Leo J. O'Donovan, "Science or Prophecy? A Discussion with Jacques Monod," *American Ecclesiastical Review* 167 (1973) 543-52.

13. Pius XII, "Humani generis," *AAS* 42 (1950) 575; ET, no. 65, p. 19.

14. Blaise Pascal, "Preface sur le traite du vide," in *Opuscules et lettres (choix)*, ed. by L. Lafuma (Paris: Aubeir, 1955) 50. My translation.

15. Max Planck, *Where Is Science Going?* (New York: W. W. Norton, 1932) 214.

16. For some testimonies see Stanley L. Jaki, "The Role of Faith in Physics," *Zygon* 2 (1967) 187-202.

17. Michael Polanyi, *The Tacit Dimension* (Garden City, NY: Doubleday, 1967) 63.

18. Werner Heisenberg, *Tradition in Science* (New York: Seabury, 1983) chapter 1.

19. George A. Lindbeck, "Theological Revolution and the Present Crisis," *Theology Digest* 23 (Winter 1975) 308-19.

20. Michael Polanyi, *Personal Knowledge* (New York: Harper Torchbooks, 1964) 207. For discussion see Avery Dulles, "Faith, Church, and God: Insights from Michael Polanyi," *Theological Studies* 45 (1984) 537-50.

21. Michael Polanyi, *Science, Faith and Society* (Chicago: University of Chicago Press, 1946) quotation from p. 49.

22. A member of the commission appointed by Pope John Paul II has interpreted the condemnations of 1616 and 1633 as having merely disciplinary, rather than doctrinal, force. See Mario d'Addio, "Alcuni fasi dell'istruttoria del processo a Galileo," *L'Osservatore Romano* (March 2, 1984) 3. Further materials are presented in Paul Poupard (ed.), *Galileo Galilei: Toward a Resolution of 350 Years of Debate, 1633-1983* (Pittsburgh: Duquesne University Press, 1987).

23. Blaise Pascal, *Pensees*, no. 313 in *The Essential Pascal*, ed. Robert J. Gleason (New York: Mentor-Omega, 1966) 124. The reflections on the two infinites in no. 43, pp. 33-40, likewise exhibit the reactions of this religious genius to the dawning scientific consciousness of the age.

AUTONOMY IS NOT ENOUGH

Lindon Eaves

The Holy Father's message is a significant step forward in the relationship between science and Christian theology because it put to an end the Catholic Church's claim to hegemony with respect to the sciences. It should now be possible for theologians and scientists to engage more openly in that "critical-dialogic cooperation" for which theologians such as Hans Küng[1] have appealed. The message has been carefully and thoughtfully crafted and shows considerable sensitivity to the spirit of science.

A crucial passage in the message is that dealing with the autonomy of science and theology : "To be more specific, both religion and science must preserve their autonomy and distinctiveness . . . Each should possess its own principles, its pattern of procedures, its diversities of interpretation and its own conclusions . . ."(M8) Similar sentiments are to be found in the writings of widely different protestant theologians. Karl Barth writes: "If theology is to be ranked as a science, and lays claim to such ranking, this does not mean it must be disturbed or hampered in its task by what is described as science elsewhere . . ."[2] Paul Tillich observes similarly: "Theology has no right and no obligation to prejudice a physical or historical, sociological or psychological, inquiry. And *no result of such an inquiry can be directly productive or disastrous for theology*"[3] (emphasis added). In the latter passage Tillich draws out the implicit danger of the principle of autonomy articulated in His Holiness' message: namely that disciplines which are completely autonomous may also insulate themselves from criticism. The drawbridge of the theological castle may have been lowered, but its walls have still to be demolished. From a scientific viewpoint, the very point of contention between science and theology has been the willingness of theology to baptize science when it is convenient but to cry "autonomy" when the scientific questions have become too threatening. As the development of the sciences bears witness, the autonomy of the various disciplines within science is at best provisional and is only respected as long as the paradigms within disciplines are productive. However, significant shifts in paradigms and greater coherence in our models of reality have often arisen at those boundaries which are most painful: for example, on the boundary between the traditional biological sciences and the newer molecular sciences, or on the boundaries between the life-sciences and the behavioral sciences. The radical reconstruction of knowledge which accompanied the molecular breakthrough, forever associated with the names of Watson and Crick, is now, forty years later, being followed by a radical and sometimes painful reconstruction of university departments. Autonomy is at best provisional and vindicated only by the intellectual productivity of the autonomous disciplines.

His Holiness' message testifies to the seriousness of the Church's engagement with the physical sciences. It is, however, arguable that the claims and interests of the physical sciences are now sufficiently remote from human life and history as to have little impact (barring nuclear holocaust) on the destiny of life of which the Church proclaims herself the protectress and mediatrix. The burning question for biologists who read the message must be: "How far is this engagement and good will to be extended to the life sciences which interact much more directly and intimately with our understanding of the nature and destiny of life?" Is the Church, through the encouragement given to her scholars, prepared to demolish the castle walls or merely to lower the draw bridge for as long as it proves painless? Is she prepared to engage biology unconditionally where it hurts most?

There is, unfortunately, some evidence to suggest that the Church's generosity towards physics and cosmology does not extend to the life sciences. A speech delivered by the Holy Father to an audience of biologists, which was given after his transmittal of the current message on the occasion of Newton's Tercentennial, gives reason to doubt that the Church is even prepared to respect the autonomy of the life sciences, let alone engage in creative and mutually critical dialogue. In a recent number of "L'Osservatore Romano" (August 28-29, 1989) the Pope is quoted as saying ". . . recent developments in our understanding of the phenomenon of twinning have helped curtail a certain tendency which considered the termination of pregnancy a justifiable medical procedure. *Such developments have also demonstrated the unacceptability in moral as well as in strictly scientific terms, of all forms of genetic manipulation.*" (Emphasis added)

The principal issue at stake here is not the use to which genetic manipulation is put, or its acceptability or otherwise. Rather, the speech presents a model system for exploring one possible form of interaction between science and theology. First, there is no obvious reason why genetic manipulation should be "unacceptable in strictly scientific terms." Indeed, it is not even clear what "scientific acceptability" is unless by it we mean "productive of scientific understanding," in which case we can certainly *conceive* of forms of genetic manipulation (they are done all the time with infra-human species) which are astonishingly productive scientifically. So the issue of whether or not to undertake genetic manipulation in humans, for scientific or therapeutic purposes, is a moral one.

This leads to the second issue: what is the connection between scientific fact at the molecular level, and judgment at the moral level? This is a more profound question which lies at the heart of the dialogue between science and theology but which is not answered honestly by the strategy of baptizing scientific data for the purposes of moral crusade, nor by the naive theological claim that moral implications can be drawn from findings at the cellular level. The question is, "What is the connection, if any, between scientific claims about specific data and theological claims about the same data?" The question was posed to me recently by another priest-biologist: "How is God present at the events of meiosis?" That is, what in reality makes it *necessary* to speak of the crucial events of reproduction – the "decision" about which forms of which genes go into which gametes – in anything other than mechanistic and statistical terms?

It seems, at first sight, that scientific and theological claims about the material facts, the events of meiosis, for example, must both lay claim to be rooted in facts, if there is to be any constructive dialogue between science and theology. However, the source of scientific claims about events, such as those of cell-division, is made on the basis of the events themselves. For the most part, science makes claims from the "bottom up." Theological claims, however, are not made out of the events themselves but from a model of reality based in a much broader context, at least that of evolution, history and culture, and, in the case of specifically Christian claims, in the context of the historical and cultural significance of the life, death and resurrection of Jesus. Such a view has been articulated very clearly in the Christological thought of Wolfhart Pannenberg. That this broader context is not made clear in the Pope's treatment of genetic manipulation leads to a number of dangerous absurdities of which the chief is the attempt to infer moral conclusions from events which, considered by themselves, are morally ambiguous. Consider the specific issue to which His Holiness alludes in his speech to geneticists. The very data that he uses to support the Church's moral position on abortion might equally be used to support methods of contraception by the prevention of implantation. If abortion, as it is currently practiced, is demonstrated to be morally unacceptable by empirical findings that individual identity in the case of monozygotic twins is established at a time *before* abortion is typically practiced, then does it imply that methods of contraception which destroy the zygote *before* that stage of development are morally acceptable?

Even those few biologists who try to draw "value" from biology itself, and this is an exercise that they themselves undertake with the greatest temerity, do so not on the basis of the molecular minutiae of life such as events at the meiotic or embryonic level, but on the basis of a much broader biological context, namely that of the whole *phenotype* (that is, the sum total of the characteristics of the individual) in dialogue with the physical and cultural ecosystem which together establish the basis for evolutionary change. What biologists would do in fear and trembling, His Holiness has presumed without pause. The inherent caution of the biologist comes not from a blunt moral or philosophical sense, but from a far more subtle appreciation of the dangers in building moral judgments on biological facts removed from their evolutionary, historical, and cultural context.

This brief case study illustrates several principles which lie at the forefront of the future dialogue between theology and science. First, the principle of autonomy is dangerous because it leads to theoretical and cultural stagnation. Science will continue its own growth whether or not theology chooses to come along for the ride. Second, biologists need to be reassured that their science is to be accorded the same sensitivity and respect that His Holiness' message has extended to physics. Third, the immediacy of biology's impact on our understanding of life presents the Church with a problem that is both pressing and challenging. Fourth, the biological facts in themselves are morally ambiguous and cannot be used as an infallible basis for shaping the future. Fifth, the Church, therefore, needs to specify more precisely the context which comprises the mainspring of her claim to speak of God, God's moral claim upon us, and God's action in the world.

Notes

1. Hans Kung, *Does God Exist?* (London: ET, 1981) 115.

2. Karl Barth, *Church Dogmatics* (Edinburgh: ET, 1975) Vol 1:1, p.8.

3. Paul Tillich, *Systematic Theology,* (London: ET, 1978) Vol 1, p.21.

CRITIQUE: THE CHURCH AND THE SCIENTIFIC COMMUNITY

G.F.R. Ellis

I applaud the general tenor of the remarks in Pope John Paul II's statement discussing *The Church and the Scientific Community: A Common Quest for Understanding.*[1] There are some specific issues that arise and are worth pursuing, of both practical and theoretical importance; in effect I aim at a critique not so much of what is said in the message but rather of what is unsaid.

The central theme of the message is:

> . . . people are seeking intellectual coherence and collaboration, and are discovering values and experiences they have in common even within their diversities . . ." (M3) There is need for dialogue between religion and science . . . in which the integrity of both religion and science is supported and the advance of each is fostered . . . (M7) We must work to build a culture and relationship . . . in which each discipline retains its integrity and yet is radically open to the discoveries and insights of the other. (M9)

As is explained in the statement, this is a project of considerable importance, because both science and religion play a fundamental role in shaping human thought and action. What does this project entail?

The first fundamental issue that arises is the basis of knowledge and the different ways of knowing. This question occurs because of the problem of the contrast between surface appearances and underlying reality; more precisely, because of the hidden nature of the physical world on the one hand, and the hidden nature of God on the other. We cannot, for example, tell simply by looking around us the nature of the chemical elements, or of the four fundamental forces of physics; nor can we tell the nature of fundamental reality (the foundation of our being) or of the ethical life in any easy manner. Indeed, there is not even any obvious proof of the existence of God. Thus a major question is: What are the methods we can use to discern the truth? This is relatively clear in science in general (although there are scientific domains where it is not so clear), but it is relatively unclear in the field of religion and ethics (as witnessed by Pilate's question: "What is truth?").

Thus in the aim of coming to understand one another, it is important that there is a recognition of different areas of interest and different kinds of knowing, with different kinds of confirmation and verification that apply in these separate areas. Each gives a pattern of understanding, and so each gives an explanation of features of the world around us of a particular kind. Science has predictive power, enabling us to understand the inanimate forces that control the natural world, and to some extent to even understand living systems and the mind; whilst religion has normative power, and gives us an understanding of our own humanity, its deepest needs and desires, as well as of the powers required to fulfill these, and of how we ought to live.[2]

The basis of knowledge in science is the idea of observations and repeatable experiments leading to predictions of the behavior of physical systems, which can be tested and verified. The basis of knowledge in religion is a combination of: (a) belief in God's word revealed in the scriptural record of the lives and understanding of the prophets (in the case of Christianity, revealed in particular in the Biblical record of the life of Christ); (b) personal experience and conviction of the presence and nature of God; and (c) acceptance of tradition and the authority of religious institutions such as the Church, and of those claiming to be religious leaders. The problem is that all these sources of religious knowledge can be shown to have led to serious errors in the past; none of them is infallible. While science has developed tests that are quite effective in exposing false belief within its domain of competence, religion has not been so effective in this enterprise.

In the end perhaps the only tests of belief (based on the sources mentioned above) that can be applied in the religious sphere are: (d) overall satisfactoriness as a system of explanation of the world and of our lives; and (e) the test, "by their fruit ye shall know them," which applies also to science and is the major way of confirming or denying what we believe. However, this leaves unanswered the question of how we decide when a system of explanation is satisfactory, or the outcome of some action is good; these too have to be based on some combination of personal conviction and belief in authority, again resulting in a potential or actual relativization of standards. Thus inevitably there is an element of subjectivity in these matters and our conclusions depend on our culture and education, as well as on our particular historical circumstances and our maturity and level of understanding, that is to say, on our wisdom.

This individuality is the basis of the wide divergence of opinions on religious matters. Yet the capacity of the human mind to critically discern the true and the good is mysterious but undeniable. Those who hold to a religious faith must believe that it is possible to discern the meaning of life and how we ought to live, however inadequately, and that over time humanity will move towards a truer understanding of religious as well as scientific issues: towards a consensus if not on ultimate meaning, at least on codes of behavior and responsibility. Indeed, one can claim that, despite all the problems and horrors that have happened in this period, humanity has taken considerable strides in ethical understanding in the last two thousand years.

This discussion points to an important prerequisite for the proposed project to succeed. It implies that each person taking part has to give up the claim to have sole access to a particular truth, or to have possession of the whole truth. It is fundamental to the philosophy of science that in principle each person has equal access to truth; the only test of any person's theory or concept is how well it models reality, insofar as we are able to test this. Any model will be partial and incomplete: some will succeed better in expressing the core nature of aspects of reality than others. None will succeed totally, for reality is more complex than any model we may offer. Thus while all models may guide us to some degree, they will also mislead to some degree. This applies equally to the models of science (physical theories, chemistry, etc.) and to the philosophies and theologies which attempt to model the metaphysical aspect of the world. Once we cease to lay claim to be the repositories of the whole truth (which, religiously speaking, is blasphemy, as it is the claim to be infallible, to be equal to God), we are open to dialogue as to the true nature of the universe in both its scientific and ethical aspects. Thus this is the prerequisite for meaningful dialogue to take place: to be open to the aspect of truth that the other has to offer. This has to hold in both the scientific and religious spheres in their inner structure, as well as in their relation to each other.

Given this prerequisite, it is by recognizing the differences of scope and method that we can move to the aim of the project:

> . . . the unity we seek . . . is not identity . . . On the contrary, unity always presupposes the diversity and integrity of its elements . . . religion and science must preserve their autonomy and their distinctiveness . . . The unprecedented opportunity we have today is for a common interactive relationship in which each discipline retains its integrity and yet is radically open to the discoveries and insights of the other. (M8-9)

Thus workers in the two areas must understand the boundaries of competence of each: "Only a dynamic relationship between theology and science can reveal those limits which support the integrity of either discipline . . ." (M14) Perhaps the biggest problem here is the tendency for some workers in either area to dismiss the other altogether, denying its value, in effect because they do not realize the boundaries of their own discipline. This, of course, has to be overcome. A critical point is that science cannot resolve the problem of determining ethical behavior. Just as religion cannot explain the forces governing atoms, science cannot determine what is a good or bad outcome of an action, because there are no scientific criteria for 'good' and 'bad'. Again, the discovery of the nature of the physical universe and its beginnings in the 'Big Bang' is one of the major triumphs of modern science; however, the question of the origin of the laws of nature which leads to this magnificent design is beyond the scope of science, despite some valiant attempts in this direction (and although some scientists apparently do not acknowledge this limitation). In the end physics is of necessity based on metaphysics (considerations which lie beyond the powers of analysis of the scientific method); hence this method can determine physical laws but not explain them in a fundamental sense.

Once the limits are recognized the way is open to explore the boundaries of each domain on the one hand, and the intriguing interaction between them on the other. Perhaps most important is the issue of whether theological methods can benefit from scientific methodology; this certainly should be explored in depth (with the likelihood of the most useful contributions coming from the social sciences, despite their ambiguities and lack of consensus). There may even be a coming together of approaches in some areas at the frontiers of science such as the issue of the origin of the universe and of physical law itself, where the controversial "anthropic principle" is one of the proposals debated in the scientific literature (without attaining any consensus).

A further aspect is the issue of the possible theological implications of scientific discoveries, for example ,as mentioned in the papal statement, how the scientific view of the origin of the universe impinges on the view of God as its creator, and how the evolutionary perspective affects the concept of human persons as the image of God. In neither case is there a contradiction, but there is a significant impact on our understanding of the process of God at work; presumably this helps us comprehend His nature and purpose. A particularly intriguing open possibility is raised by scientific discoveries about the size of the universe and the nature of the evolution of life: this leads to a tentative (and disputed) conclusion that there probably are other intelligent beings in the universe. Thus an exciting project is the search for other civilizations on other planets; while these almost certainly exist, they may be so far from us that two-way communication is not possible. If we ever discover them, this will raise profound religious issues relating to their theologies, and in particular to the scope of the Christian message for such beings. In these and other ways science raises fascinating issues for theological consideration.

In these themes we may find ". . . a drive towards convergence . . . an impressive manifestation of the unity of nature" (M6-M7), but additionally there remain some potential conflicts that arise. We need to recognize them; they do not destroy the enterprise, but will certainly exercise us as we think about them. For example, ". . . molecular biologists have probed the structure of living material . . ." (M7) in a most impressive way. The modern understanding of molecular biology raises again the age-old problem of free will, an ancient problem in the history of theology, brought to us with new force by the advent of modern science and its implied deterministic outlook (and not made more palatable by suggestions of randomness in behavior arising either from quantum theory or from chaotic behavior of complex systems). The issue of vitalism is an important part of the discussion but vitalism is not essential to resolving the problem of free will.

When confronted by such problem areas, there may be a tendency for each discipline to focus on the unsolved problems facing the other, as a way of diminishing it. It will be good to realize here that each area has such problems, but not to reject them for this reason; such problems are inevitable because of the partial nature of understanding and because of our dependence on models of reality as mentioned earlier. It is particularly worth mentioning here the problem of good and evil which in a certain sense is unresolved by theology. One way to express it is to ask, if God is loving and good, should not the concept that God made the universe imply that there is no evil in the universe, in contradiction to our observations? No deeply satisfactory answer is available; however, Christianity does provide an extremely profound answer to the problem of evil in a different sense, through the historical fact of Christ's life and the concept of sacrifice and the suffering God. On the other side, there is a considerable problem at the foundations of science, because there exist no proper foundations for mathematics (and there are other problems such as the conceptual foundations of quantum theory and the origin of the arrow of time). Such problems do not invalidate the methods of either discipline, but they do emphasize the limits of what each approach to understanding reality can achieve. Each discipline will be in a better state to approach and face the other if it first examines and acknowledges its own foundational and internal problems, thus recognizing some of its own fallibilities and limitations. While there are mysteries at the heart of religion, the same is true of science, even if it is not fashionable to admit this.

Overall, my thesis so far agrees with that of the document (the importance of dialogue for religion and science, the need to overcome the tendency to unilateral reductionism, to fear, and isolation) and raises some particular issues for the dialogue. The theme has been the nature of understanding in its different aspects. However, the flow has not been very reciprocal; mostly it has been from science to religion rather than vice versa. But the document suggests that there is an opposite stream: ". . . science develops best when its concepts are integrated into the broader human culture and its concerns for ultimate meaning and value . . . can help others realize more fully the human potentialities of their discoveries." (M13)

The first suggestion applies primarily to the sciences such as ecology which are indeed concerned closely with broader values. It is not clear that there is much payoff of the kind suggested for the harder sciences ; indeed, they seem almost to flourish most precisely when ignoring human culture, and striking out on their own with their own rigorous internal logic. However, the second point is extremely apposite: religion has the potential to assist the lives of individual scientists: "Scientists . . . will make decisions upon what ultimately gives meaning and value to their lives and to their work. This they will do well or poorly, with the reflective depth that theological wisdom can help them attain, or with an unconsidered absolutizing of their results beyond their reasonable and proper limits" (M13). This does not affect the results themselves, but how they are regarded. The overall theme here is the impact of religion not on science but on scientists, affecting how they live their lives, and so also how they conduct their science.

This leads to the second issue raised by the document: how people behave (which of course is based on how they understand). The theme is of major significance because ". . . the impact each [religion and science] has, and will continue to have, on the course of civilization and on the world itself, cannot be overestimated . . [we are the] stewards of creation." (M5)

Here there certainly is a very serious relationship between science and religion. By its nature religion passes judgement on the applications of science in terms of its effects on human welfare, for example applauding medical applications that improve human welfare but decrying the use of science to create weapons of destruction that have the potential to destroy the entire human race. It should immediately be added that the struggle for understanding of all kinds must be regarded as part of the religious aim, so pure science too can be applauded on religious grounds when it enhances our understanding of creation. Thus one must not oversimplify this relationship, which should be a real and important one affecting not only individual scientists but the way the community relates to science as a public enterprise. This is a crucial and vital role religion can play, for science by itself is amoral: it can be used for good or bad, and is indifferent to such use (except for some branches such as ecology, which in this regard draws on sources of values outside of the scientific endeavor).

However, this is at least partly a reciprocal relationship. While religion provides the basis of the judgement of consequences of scientific activity, science helps understand the consequences of our acts, which then can be evaluated ethically. This becomes increasingly important in the modern technological age, and must in the future become more and more a vital basis for obtaining the information needed to make ethical judgments. Science even thereby gives a foundation for judging some of the acts of the Church.

This issue arises in various contexts, but the particular very serious problem that arises at the present time is world population growth and its implications. Issues which are not a problem for a small group of people become problematic when the population grows to a large size. Scientific studies can easily show that a considerable number of the major problems facing the world today (for example the firewood and pollution issues, the global climatic heating, even much of the starvation) are due essentially to the size of the population (or its excessive local concentration), and are going to get much worse unless we are able to halt its growth. Indeed, in many local areas the carrying capacity of the world is already exceeded, and the total world population is at about the level that can be comfortably supported on a continuing basis. The kind of uncontrolled growth of the past, if continued, will eventually lead to major global and regional shortages (irrespective of technological progress) and consequently to exacerbated political conflict and to deprivation and starvation on a scale much larger than seen so far in human history.

Thus one of the major requirements for a peaceful future is a worldwide campaign for population control. One must be absolutely clear on this: unless this is undertaken, the population growth that will result is a major threat to the future of humanity, globally and locally. Consequently the past and present campaigns of segments of the Church against birth control must be regarded as a serious impediment to the future welfare of humanity; this stance must be judged, through its large-scale consequences as predicted by science, to have negative implications of a dire nature. Thus science provides the means to see that this is an untenable ethical position ,if we take seriously the injunction, "By their fruits ye shall know them".

This illustrates how the interaction determining the ethical nature of actions is two-way: while the consequences of science are judged on an ethical basis that must be ultimately founded in religion, the consequences of aspects of the actions of each human being, and of the Church,[3] can also be illuminated by science. Each has something to give and something to learn. If we have each given up the claim to infallibility, to always be right, each will be able to accept the strictures on their activities implied by the other: the interaction will become a very important ethical interchange, as well as a significant intellectual activity. It is not a viable stance to accept the intellectual interchange between science and religion but reject the mutual ethical involvement, for that would be a partial interaction taking neither subject seriously; indeed, it is acceptance of such mutual ethical involvement that is a test of sincerity of the project as a whole.

These comments are, essentially, my detailed notes on the address; sometimes critical, but in the main supportive. I can only applaud the main thesis, the need for a deeper and more sustained interaction between science and theology. The interaction foreseen and proposed can indeed be both exciting and important. We must encourage those willing and able to participate to do so to the best of their ability, and to communicate their feelings widely; indeed, a movement is needed to spread the concept and concern to the general public. As stated in the papal message: ". . . those . . . who are . . . both scientists and theologians could serve as a key resource. They can also provide a much-needed ministry to others struggling to integrate the worlds of science and religion . . ." (M12)

This project can contribute to the integration of human culture in the future, and can help to diminish the fragmentation that has been more dominant in the recent past. This must be in the long-term interests of humanity, through both its contribution to thought and its call to considered action.

I thank Augustine Shutte for helpful comments on an earlier draft of this document.

Notes

1. Message of Pope John Paul II published in *Physics, Philosophy and Theology: A Common Quest for Understanding*, eds. R.J. Russell, W.R. Stoeger and G.V. Coyne (Notre Dame, IN: University of Notre Dame Press, 1988).

2. In this broad sense, systems like Marxism act at least partially as a religion too; even those who claim no overt religion have, of necessity, some form of substitute in their lives. Much of the discussion applies in this case too.

3. A model for this type of interchange between science and religion was the Commission on Birth Regulation set up by Pope John XXIII and enlarged to include representatives of all the relevant sciences by Pope Paul VI. It produced a report that is a fine example of collaborative effort.

NOTE ON THE INTERFACE BETWEEN SCIENCE AND RELIGION

Fang Li Zhi

The topic of the relationship between science and religion may be especially difficult for someone like me who grew up within Chinese culture. In the whole history of Chinese literature, stretching back over two and one-half thousand years, there is almost nothing written about the relationship between science and religion. Little if anything is said as to whether the interface is one of mutual support or of conflict. This appears to be the result, as many historians have pointed out, of the general absence of any strong religious influence on traditional Chinese culture.

Nevertheless, religion has, in fact, been a component, sometimes even a rather important component, of Chinese culture. Taoism is an indigenous religion which evolved from one of China's most celebrated schools of philosophy in the sixth century B.C. The Christian Church spread into China at least as early as the seventh century A.D. Buddhism and Islam were also adopted in varying degrees by some Chinese at about the same time. Indeed, the average number of religious buildings per person in China, including Churches, temples, convents and mosques, may not be much less than that in Europe or the Middle East. Almost all the Chinese emperors of the various dynasties joined, in some fashion, in religious activities. Therefore, it would not be correct to say that religion has been absent from Chinese culture.

However, in Chinese history religion has had uniquely little influence on the scholarly community. Religious culture affected only the philosophical ideas of intellectuals, rather than their personal beliefs. For instance, even though Taoism was rather popular as a religion among ordinary people in the Tang dynasty (A.D. 618-905), the Taoist cosmology -- such as the belief that everything came from nothing -- never became a matter of religious orthodoxy among astronomers as did Aristotle's cosmology in medieval Christian Europe.

This uniquely Chinese phenomenon did not change with the coming of modern science. The Jesuit Matteo Ricci was the first person to bring European astronomy and other Western sciences to China. At the same time, he also set up mission houses and Churches in Guangzhou and Beijing. The astronomy Ricci introduced was gradually accepted by Chinese astronomers and used to replace traditional Chinese astronomy in preparing calendars. Nevertheless, the Catholic Church never became popular among scholars. This sharp contrast with the Western relationship between religion and science is revealing of the typical attitude of Chinese scholars toward religion. This attitude appears to have been formed by the Confucian tradition, which puts primary emphasis on social ethics and functions, and ignores ontology. Confucius once said: "We should show respect for the Gods, but keep a distance from them." So, although in China, as in the West, the existence of God has been debated, not many scholars in China have been involved. A typical quotation from Confucianism is: "We still have so little understanding of man, how can we understand the Gods?"

If we were interested in the interface between science and religion in Chinese culture alone, we could probably stop here. If, however, we want to study the intriguing question of the relationship between science and religion in a more universal way, then Chinese history may provide a good case study through a comparison of the development of scientific ideas in China as compared to the West. Because science is the same everywhere, the differences in the development of science in different regions, nations, and countries can only be explained by differences of cultural background. Therefore, some light may be shed on the influence of religion on science by comparing the development of science in China and in the West.

Some of these interfaces between science and religion have been positive, or mutually supportive; some have been negative, or mutually in conflict. Since several negative interfaces in the history of the relationship between science and religion are already very well known, this discussion will be limited to some evidences of positive interfaces, drawing on a parallel analysis of China and the West.

It is generally acknowledged that science would not be able to progress without presuppositions and/or preselections, which serve as the sources of original scientific induction and selection. Such presuppositions and preselections can be neither demonstrated nor deduced, in the usual scientifically acceptable sense, from the scientific materials themselves. Therefore, the choice of the preselections and the acceptance of the presuppositions depend, more or less, on the cultural environment in which the scholars live. It is precisely through this interface that religions may play an important role in the development of science.

Perhaps the most important presupposition at the base of all sciences is the understandability of nature, that is, the belief that it is possible to find answers to the questions being studied. Naturally, this presupposition appears absolutely trivial in most cases. However, in the case of questions which are not too close to our day-to-day experiences, the first task at hand is to assume, as a belief, a positive reply to the prequestion: whether the problem is, in fact, understandable. In this sense, the presupposition of understandability is very significant.

One of the key questions on which almost all generations of scholars in the West have focused is how the moon, planets, and stars are maintained in the sky and do not fall to the earth as nearby objects do. This topic was repeatedly studied, discussed, and answered by thinkers from Aristotle to Newton. Of course, from the perspective of modern physics, all the pre-Newtonian answers are incorrect. The important point to note, however, is that all of those early thinkers believed one could find the answer to this question. Facing the problem of the maintenance of celestial objects, the scholars of the West all adopted the presupposition of understandability.

The situation in China was completely different. According to Chinese literature of the third century, some Chinese in the city of Ji were worrying about whether and when the sky would collapse. In contrast to the West, this question had never attracted the serious attention of Chinese scholars. The predominant response to this question was that one cannot find any believable answers to it. The most famous poet of the Tang dynasty, Li Bai, wrote: "Why like the people of Ji waste time worrying about the collapse of the heavens?" Since then, in Chinese, "to worry about the collapse of the heavens like the people of Ji" has become an idiom to describe a person who pays attention to problems without meaning. Confronted with the problem of how celestial objects are maintained in the sky, Chinese scholars selected the presupposition of non-understandability. This strongly supports the idea that, roughly speaking, the boundaries between the presuppositions of understandability and non-understandability are culturally dependent.

Why were presuppositions so different in China and in the West? It appears that the only explanation available lies in the differences in culture. Religion contributes to precisely these kinds of cultural differences. Even though religious propositions are quite different from scientific propositions, when Western theology attempted to demonstrate what one should and can do in the study of religious propositions, theology itself also adopted the presupposition of understandability in its system. In theology there were many traditional propositions, such as the existence of God, which are even more transcendental than the problem of the maintenance of celestial objects. Therefore it was natural, given such a religious tradition, that there were only a few skeptics who doubted the possibility of finding a solution to the problem of the maintenance of celestial objects. The presupposition of understandability came, at least in part, from the Western religious traditions. In this sense, the presupposition that problems which are remote from direct experiences or even transcendental are nonetheless understandable was an interface between science and religion in the West. And it was a positive interface.

The second contrast between the ancient astronomies of China and the West concerns the movement of the planets. All the orbits of stars in the celestial sphere are regularly circular. However, the five planets visible to the naked eye in our solar system are exceptional and abnormal, seen from the earth. The planets do not appear to move regularly in their circuit across the sky; they seem to be moving at times more slowly and at times more quickly, sometimes even retrogressing and coming to a stop between these two movements. These phenomena had been recorded with about the same precision by both Chinese and Western astronomers. Both astronomies had their own methods to predict the planetary movements, including the retrograde motion and the stops.

The difference between ancient Chinese astronomy and its Western counterpart was that the latter was always concerned with explaining away the apparent abnormalities and anomalies in the movements of the planets, while the former was not. A key issue in Western astronomy was to develop a model to show that the movements of the stars and the planets were, actually or intrinsically, uniform with one other. To search for such uniformity among the stars and the planets was a common pursuit in the Western astronomical community. This was an important basis by which Copernicus was motivated to establish the theory of heliocentricity, in which all celestial objects move regularly along their circular orbits, and the stoppings, retrogressions, and progressions of the planets are not their own, but are a reflection of the movement of the earth. In a word, confronted with differences in the movements of stars and planets, Western astronomers adopted the presupposition of uniformity.

In contrast, Chinese astronomers showed themselves to be more interested in abnormal phenomena. In ancient Chinese astronomy, one can find many more records than in the West of abnormal objects, such as meteors, comets, sun spots, nova and supernova. Chinese astronomers were, in fact, more willing to adopt the schema of diversifications. It was also, therefore, quite natural that, under this schema, Chinese astronomers never considered that the differences in the movements of stars and planets were any more crucial than other abnormal phenomena recorded.

The different responses to the same planetary problems by Chinese and Western astronomies probably resulted in part from the different religious traditions in their respective cultures. Western and, in particular, Christian religious doctrines affirmed that the whole universe was created by one Creator. Such a view may foster astronomical theories of uniformity. Taoism similarly supports uniformity in this extreme form. In the classic *Tao-Te Ching*, for example, it is written that: "The one produced the two, the two produced the three, and the three produced all things in the universe." Nevertheless, as previously mentioned, Taoism, unlike Confucianism, did not become the dominant ideology in Chinese culture.

We can, therefore, conclude that the presupposition of uniformity is a second important interface between science and religion. The absolute faith in uniformity in the West may be the reason that Western astronomy failed to record some abnormal celestial objects. However, with regard to unmasking the mystery of planetary movements, the presupposition of uniformity was surely a positive interface between science and religion in the West.

The concept of relativity provides a third example in the contrast between Chinese and Western patterns of the interface between science and religion. A very well-known passage in Galileo's *Dialogue Concerning the Two Chief World Systems* states:

> Shut yourself up . . . in the main cabin below decks on some large ship . . . Have a large bowl of water with some fish in it . . . With the ship standing still . . . the fish swim indifferently in all directions. When you have observed . . . carefully . . . have the ship proceed at any speed you like, so long as the motion is uniform . . . You will discover not the least change . . . nor could you tell . . . whether the ship was moving or standing still.

This passage is generally recognized as the first time in the history of physics that the concept of relativity was touched upon. Indeed, this passage played an important role in the establishment of Galileo's principle of inertia, of Newton's mechanics, and even of Einstein's relativity.

It is very interesting to note that an almost identical statement can be found in the Chinese literary work *Shang Shu Wei*, which preceded Galileo's *Dialogue* by more than a thousand years. *Shang Shu Wei* said:

> The Earth is constantly in motion, while man feels nothing,
> like a person who stays in a moving cabin.

The aim of this statement appears to be identical to that of Galileo, who wanted to respond to those who asked why we feel nothing, if the earth is moving at high speed, with an explanation provided by the theory of terrestrial motion. This idea in *Shang Shu Wei* did not, however, have any impact on the development of physical concepts in China. One of the famous Chinese scholars living at the same time as Galileo, Fang Yizhi, wrote the first Chinese book to introduce some of Galileo's results, entitled *Essay on Physics*. In his book, Fang Yizhi only mentioned the *Shang Shu Wei* statement on relativity in an unimportant footnote.

The difference in the responses to the concept of relativity in China and the West is related to the absence of the concept of universality in China's traditional sciences. Since there was no belief in the existence of universal principles, and no motivation to find universal laws in Nature, the statements about "feeling nothing in a moving cabin" were then of no special significance, but only limited metaphors or analogies used to explain "feeling nothing of the earths motion." However, Galileo's statement was based on an implicit presupposition: celestial physics is not different from terrestrial physics. This was the presupposition of universality. Many events in the history of physics had already demonstrated that universal principles could be arrived at gradually by analyzing some specific analogy, as in the method of ideal experiments. Such successes could only be reached under the influence of the presupposition of universality. We cannot say that the concept of universality is entirely due to Western religious traditions, since the concept was so splendidly developed in ancient Greece. Nevertheless, Western religious culture did maintain and strengthen both the belief in the existence of universal principles and the enthusiasm to seek universality in the universe. Therefore, the principle of universality can also be categorized as another example of a positive interface between science and Western religion.

One preliminary result of this parallel analysis is that the claim for a dichotomy between scientific and religious cultures becomes far less impressive. The interfaces between both communities can clearly be seen first at the point of the formation, acceptance, or rejection of presuppositions and preselections in scientific activities. Indeed, human civilization is a whole; it is inseparable in the sense that each part in this whole will inevitably interact with others and each part can contribute to other parts. If one looks carefully at the construction of scientific theories, it becomes evident that collaboration and interaction among the various components in human civilization, including science and religion, are both important and necessary.

RESPONSE TO THE MESSAGE OF JOHN PAUL II ON THE RELATIONSHIP BETWEEN THE SCIENTIFIC AND RELIGIOUS CULTURES OF OUR TIMES

Elizabeth A. Johnson, CSJ

In our times several powerful, long-standing hostilities are beginning to thaw, as evidenced by dialogue and new cooperation among the Christian Churches, between these Churches and the major religions of the world, between the political blocs of East and West, and between traditionally warring parties in Asia. As part of this move, however lurching, toward the dream of one world it is welcome, indeed, to have a message which officially sounds a truce, at least from one side, between religious and scientific intellectual endeavors, all too often marked by mutual incomprehension and suspicion. As an irenic yet urgent call to mutual interaction which will lead to constructive relations between these two communities of inquiry, this message is excellent.

The most valuable aspect of this message, apart from its very existence, is its vision of the unity that could exist between these two communities of knowing. In this vision neither science nor religion loses its distinctiveness; neither is reduced to the other. Rather, each retains its own integrity in a dynamic interchange which leads to new mutual respect, new reciprocal enrichment, and new possibilities of contributing together to the good of humanity. The common interactive relationship itself becomes a reality embracing both communities in their diversity: "We are asked to become one. We are not asked to become each other" (M8).

Such a view of mutual relatedness which preserves integrity precludes at the outset any temptation of one enterprise to impose its truth upon the other. Thus it may allay fears that justifiably arise from the painful history of science and religion in the last half millennium. It further curbs any tendency for one discipline to approach the other simplistically, oblivious to real differences and overly optimistic about an easy harmony. Rejecting the blind alleys of both dominance and facile concordance, the concept of unity powerfully conveyed in this message has the potential to galvanize efforts toward mutual dialogue and cooperation, not only for science and religion but for any communities inching toward peace.

One omission in the message stands out as persistently curious, since its inclusion would have greatly strengthened the message's critical persuasive power. While mention is made of 'crisis' in a generic way, no explicit notice is taken of the severe ecological crisis now plaguing the fragile envelope of life and its support systems on earth. Both science and religion are guilty of contributing to the creation of this crisis. Advancements in practical science have made it possible to poison the soil and air, deplete the ozone layer, pollute the waters, acidify the rain, and kill off species of nonhuman creatures at a violent rate. For centuries this was not countered but supported by western Christianity's interpretation of the creation story in Genesis, which placed human beings in a position of dominion over the earth with the charge to subdue it. Now scientists are in the vanguard of those sounding the tocsin, and theologians are rediscovering resources in Scripture and tradition which call for reverence and responsible stewardship in face of the earth and its creatures. The ecological crisis is both a theoretical and practical situation replete with danger for the future of humanity. When the life support systems of earth are gone or sufficiently damaged, so too will be the living beings who depend on them. Here science and religion already find themselves with a critically important common goal, about which there is no dispute, and to which each is able to contribute distinct resources. Working both in theory and practice toward the overriding purpose of preserving life on earth they would find themselves to be good partners. Had this message addressed the step most obviously ready to hand for the significant advancement of relations between the scientific and religious cultures, it would have given teeth to its vision.

In a series of provocative questions the message points to developments in theology which might follow from a dialogue with contemporary science (M11). To these questions about the understanding of creation, theological anthropology, Christology, eschatology, and theological method I would add two more. How does dialogue with contemporary science affect theology's understanding of the scope of its own task? And how does this conversation affect the concepts of God and God's relation to the world?

Whatever modern sensibilities may consider its deficits, classical theology to its credit was strong in the universality of its purview. The totality of reality as the creation of the one God was the horizon as well as a subject of its reflection. This universal mindset is captured in stone in the great medieval cathedrals. There all manner of creatures in the heavens and on the earth are portrayed: natural phenomena such as wind and fire, human phenomena of crafts and skills, even Satan and his legions, all are included in the universe of the one universal God. The anthropocentrism of the theology of recent centuries, influenced by the modern philosophical turn to the subject, is a departure from this long tradition of biblical, patristic, and medieval times. It has resulted in loss of a cosmic vision in much western theology. Dialogue with contemporary cosmologies can restore such a realization, not to the detriment of recent insights into the value of the human person but in a new synthesis. Through such conversation theology will be pushed to rediscover the universality of its task, to think about all beings both in their uniqueness and their unbroken continuity with all others in the light of God, and to give an account of the whole world as God's creation. With interpretation of the cosmos once again forming a horizon of thought, ancient themes such as the play of the Holy Spirit in the world, the cosmic scope of the salvation effected in Christ, and the universal meaning of the resurrection can come into view in a new way.

The understanding of God and God's relation to the world presented by classical theism is another area susceptible to benefit from dialogue with science. Already under question for many other reasons, including the shift away from Greek philosophy and the experience of massive suffering in this century, the concept of a God without real relation to the world, a God who acts on the world by direct intervention, a God who "allows" evil to happen, and who remains unaffected by the historical process is increasingly out of step with some of the most profound assumptions of the contemporary mind. New scientific views of the cosmos, its coming into being and the forces by which it operates, are already giving rise to a new vision of God in relation to the world. This involves a unitive framework rather than a dualistic one, and reaches new frontiers in the Christian imagination of God and God's acts. Traditional views of divine attributes such as omnipotence and impassibility and of doctrines such as providence are being rethought as a result. There are ways of thinking that we do not yet know, and theology is only at the beginning stages of this process. I do not know of anyone who has yet come to a coherent vision of God in relation to the new science of chaos, for example. But the fruitfulness of a vigorous dialogue with science is unquestionable for new understandings of the relation of the natural world, humanity and God, and even for the doctrine of God in itself.

Stepping back from the message itself and pondering its wider impact, one can only cheer it on and hope its influence will be profound. The suspicion arises, however, that other factors may dilute its usefulness. In particular a monolithic view of what constitutes religious culture runs through this message. This does not take practically into account the diversity of religions and especially of Christian theologies in dialogue with science. Given the history of hierarchial authorities with theologians, both ancient and recent, one wonders if it would indeed be "safe" today for a theologian to explore the intersection of new scientific insight with religious tradition apart from clearly delineated, pre-given areas of inquiry. The message in its ecclesial context seems to be an instance of the cordiality which is extended to the former enemy or stranger but which is not similarly extended to the faithful family member who speaks in a different voice. The genuine excellence of this message and its vision of interactive unity between science and religion would be more credible and even more powerful if its principles were applied to dialogue about new insights within the community of faith itself as well as to conversation *ad extra*.

CRITIQUE OF THE MESSAGE OF HIS HOLINESS POPE JOHN PAUL II

Malu wa Kalenga

Introduction

In spite of their rather tumultuous relationship in the past, His Holiness Pope John Paul II, in his message, is of the opinion that science and theology can have a fruitful and meaningful dialogue.[1] This optimistic assessment is grounded on the new *esprit du temps*, to which the Holy See has contributed immensely. It is also supported by the fact that twentieth century theoretical models in physics, particularly in quantum mechanics and in cosmology, involve a number of philosophical connotations. With philosophy playing the middle ground, it is assumed that theology and the natural sciences can interact in such a way as to gain a ". . . more thorough understanding of one another's disciplines . . ." (M4) Such understanding will permit each discipline ". . . to enrich, nourish and challenge the other to be more fully what it can be . . ." (M7)

The level of the dialogue between science and theology that Pope John Paul II is advocating is a very deep one. Obviously, it has to go far beyond a "heuristic theology",[2] which concerns itself with the use of metaphors and models adopted from the natural sciences for apologetical purpose.

Is such a deep level interaction between the natural sciences and theology really possible today or in the foreseeable future? If yes, under what conditions? These are the questions we wish to consider in the following comments on His Holiness Pope John Paul II's message. Also, because one can consider theology and philosophy as falling into the broad category of the social sciences, we must consider as well the wider problem raised by the deep interaction between the social and the natural sciences.

The Need of a Deep Level Dialogue

As a scientist and as a Catholic I find myself in complete agreement with His Holiness Pope John Paul II's call for a meaningful dialogue between the culture of religious belief and the culture of science. Such a dialogue is important because the two cultures have a ". . . major influence on the development of ideas and values . . ." in the world (M2). They interact, although mainly in an informal way, to shape the course of humanity. They are major components of the human culture. It is, therefore, advisable to formalize their interaction in order to bring them more efficiently into support of each other. This mutual support is crucial in the effort to eliminate the ". . . separation between truth and values . . ." (M2) that tends to prevail in modern society.

This latter task is an important one, for the widening disparity between the material and the nonmaterial dimensions of modern culture is dangerous. It has the effect of rendering the issue of development more and more complex, particularly in the Third World. While science and technology contribute, at a quickening pace, to the improvement of the material well-being of the human race, social ills keep cropping up, poisoning international relations. This is happening in spite of various prescriptions that are given, but which seem to generate more ill feeling and debate than good solutions. It is becoming urgent to bring social and natural scientists together in a different fashion than what has been tried before, in order to make them work together more effectively to promote a more human world, where values and truth will no longer be separated.

Is a Deep Level Dialogue Possible?

Unfortunately, the dialogue between the social and natural sciences is constrained by many factors. In his message Pope John Paul II dwells on some that concern theology specifically, where theology is defined as "an effort of faith to achieve understanding". He asks the following question: "Can theological method fruitfully appropriate insights from scientific methodology and the philosophy of science?" (M11).

Such an appropriation will certainly render the dialogue between theology and the natural sciences more meaningful. But it cannot be carried out without first devising a suitable paradigm, at a suitable hierarchical level, to help encompass the methodologies of both social and natural sciences. This entails a reconceptualization of the natural sciences, and possibly of theology as well.[3]

We propose to find out if such a reconceptualization of the natural sciences is possible, and if it can be conceived as an extrapolation, or an enlargement, of the thoughts and perspectives that underlie the quantum formalism. For that purpose it is necessary to specify the dialogue problematic between the social and the natural sciences.

The Dialogue Problematic

To understand God, nature, or the complex global problems of development, the early scientific reductionistic approach which relied on a single discipline of learning has long been replaced by a holistic approach, such as the now common interdisciplinary undertaking. Often, however, approaches considered interdisciplinary are actually merely multidisciplinary.[4]

This is because the plurality in values, interests and methodologies also means that in practice there are irreconcilable differences in the views expressed by different disciplines of learning. The critical openness, the vital and mutual interchange, called for by His Holiness Pope John Paul II as far as theology and the natural sciences are concerned, are thus very difficult, at least at the deep level that will constitute a truly mutual enrichment for the disciplines involved.

A two-way enrichment is only possible if one is able to transform a multidisciplinary undertaking into a truly interdisciplinary one. One method to achieve this is the interpardigmatic dialogue.[5] For an interparadigmatic dialogue to be really fruitful a natural consensus must exist at a suitable hierarchical level among the disciplines involved. That is, they must share, at some suitable higher level, the same major principles of conjunction and disconjunction.

The need of a common paradigm at a suitable higher hierarchical level arises first because interparadigmatic dialogue is constrained by a high fragmentation of knowledge which renders communication very difficult amongst scientists even of the same discipline, let alone between social and natural scientists. Furthermore, members of an interparadigmatic group address different aspects of a given problem, with different tools, different conceptualizations, different criteria as to what constitutes the truth, and finally differences in the degree of confidence in their findings.

The difficulty of the interparadigmatic dialogue is compounded by the fact that a difference in the addressed aspect of a problem means in practice a difference in the perceived complexity of the system being considered. Indeed, the complexity of a system resides in the eye of the observer. It is, therefore, very difficult for a social scientist to adopt from classical science without modification its methodological principles and criteria for evaluation of the truth, since they call for, among other things, extracting the observer from the observed. On the other hand, to renounce the exacting discipline and methodology of classical science, which has demonstrated tremendous success, is to confine social sciences to the uncertain value of a simple rhetorical science.

Finally, the interparadigmatic approach does not suppress the fact that the social scientists find themselves ill at ease in a world where physics, since the Newtonian revolution, defines the laws of nature as being fundamentally deterministic and reversible.

As seen from the above discussion, bringing together scholars from the social and natural sciences for a meaningful dialogue is a difficult task. It is not, however, a hopeless one.[6] Niels Bohr and quantum formalism can be shown to play an important role in support of this statement.[7]

The Feasibility of a New Scientific Paradigm

The history of science and the study of the evolution of the paradigms that underlie scientific thinking show clearly a global shift, over the years, of concepts such as determinism, causality, time, order, certainty, and divisibility.[8] One comes slowly to the realization that there is a natural limit to our ability to improve our information about nature; that uncertainty and chance are integral parts of the universe.

The shift started with the introduction of chance, first in biology with Darwin and the post-Darwinians, then in thermodynamics with Bolzman, Gibbs and Fowler. It has gained more ground since the first half of the twentieth century, starting with the celebrated Heisenberg uncertainty principle and the statistical interpretation of Schroedinger's wave function by Born in quantum mechanics[9]; then with the intrusion of physics in biology; and finally with the discovery in many disciplines of learning in the natural sciences of processes and systems that display behavior that closely resemble the evolutionary and nondeterministic behavior of living organisms.[10] Recent scientific evidence in many fields, ranging from biology to ecology and economics suggests at least one tentative statement: determinism and reversibility do not constitute by themselves fundamental laws of nature. To apprehend reality one must incorporate the concepts of chance and of irreversibility alongside those of determinism and reversibility.[11]

This suggests that the most suitable scientific paradigm is the one that makes way for the introduction of the logic of inclusion, or conjunction, along with the logic of exclusion, or disjunction, that has been at the core of classical science since the Newtonian revolution.[12] Such a paradigm, if it is possible to devise one, will help the development of more effective models and tools of scientific investigation, and will permit us to take into account more fruitfully the basic facts emerging in the natural as well as in the social sciences. Some of those facts are as follows:

a. The observer is no longer completely outside the system being observed.[13]

b. The concept of isolated or closed systems, composed of entities behaving like automata, pursuing predictable rational paths, is at best a crude approximation of reality.[14]

c. At the macro level one is more likely to deal with open systems subject to the flow of energy, matter and information, following an essentially evolutionary and adaptive course, punctuated by essentially undeterministic choice, and thus more or less indeterministic behavior.[15]

d. There exists an hierarchy of relations and interactions between the pertinent key factors of a given system. This hierarchy can be used to explain the past but not necessarily all the future paths that the system will take or can follow because of the "noise" in the system. This "noise" is tied not only to the presence of the "choice" factor, which instills uncertainty in the development process of the system, but also to the basic uncertainty underlying the interaction process itself.[16]

e. The decision or choice process in a given system is not truly free but is dependent: on the interplay between internal and external circumstances; on the emerging collective values and their relative acceptability; on the weight of the past; on the anticipated value or usefulness of a possible future; on the adaptive response to anticipated consequences of today's decisions.[17]

f. Many systems, at the micro level as well as in the macro level, display long distance correlations that undermine the assumption of unlimited divisibility found in classical science.[18]

The above considerations show that one can not rely only on the physical laws of conservation of energy, mass, momentum, and charge of classical physics to model the complex systems one encounters in various fields of study, including physico-chemistry, social sciences, and biology.

One is thus confronted with questions like the following:

How to situate, and thus to be able to model, complex systems, including social and biological ones, with regard to the general laws or organizations of natural sciences.[19]

How to integrate chance and determinism in order to explain, and thus, hopefully, to be able to model, the development of biological and social structures.[20]

The old position that consisted of simply discarding the problem by assuming that there is a basic separation between living and nonliving systems is no longer acceptable. Choice and freedom can be visualized in physical systems, as for example in many dissipative structures.[21]

It is therefore necessary to ascertain the feasibility of an all embracing scientific paradigm in which the following conjunctions of concepts which appear antinomical can be integrated: (a) conjunction of the observer and of the observed; (b) conjunction of reversibility and of irreversibility; (c) conjunction of certainty and of uncertainty; (d) conjunction of separability and of nonseparability; (e) conjunction of order and of disorder; (f) conjunction of equilibrium and of nonequilibrium; (g) conjunction of the stable and of the unstable; (h) conjunction of the project and of the situation.

Some of the conjunctions listed can be viewed as applications of ideas introduced by Bohr. Others can be related to well known results and paradoxes of quantum mechanics.[22] The problem one is confronted with here is to know if the new emerging ideas and views of the importance of chance, uncertainty, and adaptive behavior which seem to characterize many scientific disciplines can truly lead to some kind of unification of the sciences through the formulation, at an appropriate hierarchical level, of a new scientific paradigm that will encompass concepts that are antinomical. That such a formulation is desirable has, I hope, been made sufficiently clear in the above discussion. It follows, not only from the discovery of new complex systems in many fields of learning, but also from the necessity to insure a deep, meaningful dialogue between the social sciences and the natural sciences that will help to diminish the increasing separation between values and truth that pervades modern society.

Conclusion

To carry out the thorough-going dialogue between theology and the natural sciences that Pope John Paul II is advocating is a difficult task. The dialogue between the social and natural sciences cannot take place at the deep level required unless a suitable common paradigm is devised. The feasibility of such a paradigm is doubtful at the present time, but not hopeless.

For the foreseeable future the linguistic problem between theology and the natural sciences will remain. It will possibly grow in the future, since theoretical models in some branches of physics, such as cosmology, are becoming more and more complex.

The most that can be achieved at the present time is the appropriation by theology of some credible models of the natural sciences for apologetical purposes. This is at most a one-way "consonance" between theology and science that hopefully can introduce some kind of "coherence of worldview."[23] To go deeper than that, at the present time, raises the risk of making the concepts of physics normative for theology. The increasing speculative character of theories and models in some branches of physics, such as cosmology, renders this route undesirable.

Notes

1. See editorial notes on the page of Contents.

2. Sallie McFague, "Models of God for an Ecological, Evolutionary Era: God as Mother of the Universe," in *Physics,Philosophy and Theology: A Common Quest for Understanding*, eds. R.J. Russell, W.R. Stoeger, and G.V. Coyne (Notre Dame, IN: University of Notre Dame Press, 1988) 250.

3. Such a possible reconceptualization of theology will have to go far beyond the "hypothetical consonance" of Ted Peters, "On Creating the Cosmos," in *Physics, Philosophy, and Theology: A Common Quest for Understanding, op. cit.*, p. 274.

4. Urban Youssan, "The Socio-Economic Causes of Hunger," in *Food as a Human Right*, eds. Asbjorn Eide et al. (Tokyo:United Nations University (UNU) Publication, 1984) 22-36.

5. J. Galtung, *Goals, Processes, and Indicators of Development: A Project Description* (Tokyo:UNU Publication, 1978).

6. See for example: I. Prigogine and E. Stengers, *La Nouvelle Alliance* (Gallimard, 1979).

7. Malu wa Kalenga, "Epistémologie, Physique et Developpement: l'Influence de Niels Bohr" in *Recherches Nucléaires et Développement du Zaire*, ed.Malu wa Kalenga (Zaire:Presse du C.G.E.A., 1986).

8. See amongst others: Max Born, *Natural Philosophy of Cause and Chance* (Dover Publications, 1964) and *Experiment and Theory in Physics* (Dover Publications, 1956); Niels Bohr, *Physique et Connaissance Humaine* (Gonthier, 1961).

9. See note 8.

10. See amongst others: I. Prigogine, "En Guise d'introduction: Un Monde à Découvrir," *Nouvelles de la Science et de la Technique*, 2 (1984) 5-11; P.M. Allen, "The Evolutionary Paradigm of Dissipative Structures," in *The New Evolutionary Vision, AAA Selected Symposiums*, ed. E. Yantsh (Boulder,CO:Westview Press, 1981).

11. See amongst others: Aida et al., *The Science and Praxis of Complexity* (United Nations University (UNU), 1985); I. Prigogine and E. Stengers, *Entre le Temps et l'Éternité* (Fayard, 1988).

12. J.P. Lemoigne, "The Intelligence of Complexity," in *The Science and Praxis of Complexity*, *op.cit*, see note 11, pp. 35-61.

13. Niels Bohr, *op. cit.*, see note 8, p. 34.

14. I. Prigogine, "New Perspectives on Complexity," in *The Science and Praxis of Complexity*, *op. cit.*, pp. 107-118.

15. I. Prigogine and E. Stengers, *Physique, Temps et Devenir* (Masson, 1982).

16. P.M. Allen, *op. cit.*, see note 10.

17. See, for example, various papers in *The Science and Praxis of Complexity, op. cit.*, see note 11.

18. As shown by the Aspects's experiment in the framework of the Einstein-Podolski-Rosen argument (see for example Malu wa Kalenga, *op. cit.*, see note 7). For macro systems, see amongst others: P.M. Allen, *op. cit.*, see note 10; *The Science and Praxis of Complexity, op. cit.*, see note 11.

19. "For we all think, in accord with Newton, that science is based on the certitude that nature always obeys the same laws in the same conditions." Niels Bohr, *op. cit.*, see note 8, p. 19.

20. The problem here concerns the conditions of observation in physics, in biology, and in the social sciences, namely how and where to establish the clear-cut distinction between the "subject" and the "object" of a scientific investigation that allows the universal use of the universal concepts of classical physics, necessary for the univocal and universal communication of the results of the observation. According to Bohr (*op. cit.*, see note 8, pp. 66, 148, 164), the distinction is fixed in classical mechanics, and depending on the "free will" in human sciences such as psychology.

21. See amongst others: G. Nicolis, "Bifurcation, Fluctuations and Dissipative Structures," in *Nonlinear Phenomena in Physics and Biology*, eds. R.H. Enns et al. (Plenum Press, 1981) 185-208; G. Nicolis, "Irreversible Thermodynamics," in *Rep. Prog. Physics* 42 (1979) 227-267; I. Prigogine and G. Nicolis, "Self Organization in Nonequilibrium Systems: Toward a Dynamics of Complexity," in M. Hazwinkel et al., *Bifurcation Analysis* (Reidel Publishing, 1985) 3-12; P. Allen, *op. cit.*, see note 10.

22. Malu wa Kalenga, *op. cit.*, see note 7.

23. Ernan McMullin, "How Should Cosmology Relate to Theology?" in *The Sciences and Theology in the Twentieth Century*, ed. A.R. Peacocke (Notre Dame, IN: University of Notre Dame Press, 1980).

THE CHURCH AND THE SCIENTIFIC COMMUNITIES

Cardinal Carlo Maria Martini

The message, "The Church and the Scientific Communities: a Common Quest for Understanding", deals with the conviction that between science and faith, and in particular between the scientific community and the Church, there should be a substantial convergence, while each of the two maintains its own proper specific identity.   This conviction, which is expressed in the invitation extended in a special way to theologians and scientists ". . . to intensify their constructive relations of interchange through unity" (M14) does not, however, ignore the complex nature of the problems which must be confronted. The question of the relationship between science and faith has, in fact, many aspects which often overlap and are interwoven.

The question has, above all, a troubled past which, since the end of the Middle Ages, with the establishment of modern science, continues to some degree to have an impact. The misunderstandings and conflicts which have characterized this history have solidified prejudices between the two parties: the Church has been led to judge the sciences as dangerous to faith and, from the other side, the scientific community has been led to hold the Church responsible for obstructing progress in scientific research.

The key in this historical controversy is principally of a theoretical nature, that is, the relationship between the "truth" of the faith and the "truth" of the sciences.   It has frequently shown itself as a relationship between irreconcilable alternatives, thus causing individuals to face excruciating, unresolvable choices.

In fact, today the Church is aware – this document is an authoritative indication of that awareness – that such apparent antagonism is usually due to an inadequate understanding of the epistemological underpinnings of the faith, on the one hand, and of the sciences on the other. This antagonism arises when one is led in the end to hold as divine revelation convictions and opinions which, in fact, are expressions of the culture of a given age, and which are employed by Christian thought, even in Biblical texts, only as a linguistic tool to express religious truth. Objectively, this linguistic tool has a more or less contingent character, and this is especially true with respect to the simplicity of its view of natural phenomena.

On the other hand, proponents of modern science have often been inclined to make exorbitant claims for the scientific method, attributing to it exhaustive and incontrovertible explanations of reality. At the risk, to some extent always present, of an unwarranted intrusion into the other's area of competence, a remedy may be found through a reciprocal critical evaluation made possible by a more intense dialogue between the Church and the scientific community: "What is important, as we have already stressed, is that the dialogue should continue and grow in depth and scope. In the process we must overcome every regressive tendency to a unilateral reductionism, to fear, and to self-imposed isolation" (M7). "Science can purify religion from error and superstition; religion can purify science from idolatry and false absolutes" (M13).

If past events have urged us on to a clarification on the theoretical level, expectations for the future confront both the Church and the scientific community with a common responsibility of a practical nature. Progress in the sciences and, above all, in technological developments which accompany that progress, is a factor which once again poses, with exceptional urgency and seriousness, the ethical question, that is, the question of the "good life".

From this point of view, the question of ecology may be symptomatic of the age in which we live. Contrary to the promise of a future finally free from every need – such was the hope that accompanied the birth and rapid success of modern science – it appears that science constitutes an outright threat to the conditions for human life, not only the material ones (water, soil, flora, and fauna), but also, and perhaps more importantly, those which are cultural: "So much of our world seems to be in fragments, in disjointed pieces" (M2). The fragmentation of which John Paul II speaks is also an effect of changes which have their driving force in the sciences and which, through technological and economic factors, have an influence which compromises the quality of coexistence in society. The enormous power at the disposition of modern science and technology cannot be left to itself but, in so far as possible, must be controlled and directed. This is surely a difficult task, but it is a decisive one. It calls for a response both from the believer and the scientist.

However, for a more precise determination of such a response, it would be well to distinguish two different aspects and levels of that which is currently meant by the term, science. This term, above all, designates a particular method of coming to a knowledge of truth and reality, a method whose paradigm is found in the exact natural sciences. Its theoretical elements, including axioms, hypotheses, and theories, and its practical procedures, based on observation and experimentation, prescind purposely from subjective aspects, such as the needs and propensities of the researcher, but also from value judgments and convictions about the significance of reality. The essential aim of this method of knowing is to discover, in the realm of the factual, the laws which interconnect the various phenomena of the reality being investigated.

In this first meaning of the term a scientific assertion may be right or wrong, true or false; but there is no obvious way in which it is susceptible to moral judgment. Thus understood, prescinding from the historical-social context in which, in fact, it is embedded, science is "value free".

On the other hand, we must judge in a quite different way science concretely understood as a subsystem of society, that is, as an activity endowed with specific institutions which interact with other activities and their institutions: economics, the arts, politics, religion, etc. In this second meaning of the term, science is not a neutral reality from the point of view of values. It is rather oriented by well determined interests and choices not simply reducible to intellectual curiosity. Think only of the large financial investment, required to carry out scientific research. Many times, to the detriment of other needs, funds are made available to research by economic and political powers whose aims can be quite different from those of science. The very person who decides to devote time and effort to scientific research, and above all selects the particular field of research to be pursued, does not do so for reasons which are exclusively scientific in the proper sense of the term.

Science, therefore, as a personal and social activity, is part of a much larger complex with which there is a continuous interplay. Only by considering such relationships do we see the true meaning and value of science, that is, the contribution which it effectively brings, for better or for worse, to the quality of human life. From this point of view an ethical judgment on science is not only legitimate but even inescapable.

Precisely because of the ethical issues raised these days by science, the Church feels herself involved, as the message of John Paul II indicates. In fact, the Church cannot fail to accept the role of giving its own contribution to a more adequate understanding of what the "good life" means and what the conditions are for its fulfillment. This role of the Church is expressed in various ways as is shown *in actu exercito* by this very pontifical document. Above all, in the face of tendencies, processes, and positions which are negative and dangerous, the Church must keep a critical vigilance. In a world as complex as today's, it is not always easy to name precisely the threats which weigh upon the future of humanity. We need a clear capacity of discernment so that we can understand phenomena and foresee how they will develop before they produce disastrous results.

On the other hand, such discernment is possible because the Church draws from the faith invaluable indications of how to define the horizons of meaning within which to situate and, consequently, to interpret the partial moments, among which are found scientific and technological research. In fact, Christian faith, in its search to answer the ultimate questions concerning the meaning of reality, seeks to define that part of reality which corresponds to the understanding of oneself as a human being, by enlightening the self as to its position in the world, its relationship with the non-human element in the world, and the dignity and responsibility which must characterize its relationship both to other human beings and to nature itself.

Today's Church can make precious use even of past differences with the culture of the natural sciences, whose proponents find right in the chapters of Genesis a special and celebrated point of controversy. The Church can now read again the first pages of Genesis with eyes more acute, and can intuit – without confusing content with linguistic ways of presenting the content – the eternal truths to which it bears witness: the dignity of humankind as God's partner, to whom God Himself has entrusted the care of all that He has created, so that it might host the whole of humanity and be a sign which speaks of God's eternal blessing.

A COMMON QUEST FOR UNDERSTANDING

Ernan McMullin

Pope John Paul II's recent declaration on the relations of science and religion may well be the most important Roman statement on this topic since Pius XII's address to the Pontifical Academy of Sciences in 1951. The occasion is the publication of the papers from a conference on "Our Knowledge of God and Nature", held at Castel Gandolfo in 1987 to mark the third centenary of the appearance of Newton's epochal *Philosophiae Naturalis Principia Mathematica*, the founding work of modern mechanics. The Pope's letter to the participants in that conference serves as preface to the volume. It deserves, and will undoubtedly receive, wide notice.

The main theme of the Pope's remarks is the interdependence of science and religion: "We need each other to be what we must be, what we are called to be" (M14). Each can help to define the limits of the other, " . . . so that theology does not profess a pseudo-science and science does not become an unconscious theology" (M14). Scientists cannot isolate themselves from wider human concerns for ultimate meaning and value, yet their own methods are not designed to deal with such concerns. They must, therefore, look beyond those methods and techniques, and devote to this quest ". . . something of the energy and care that they give to their research in science . . . Science can purify religion from error and superstition; religion can purify science from idolatry and false absolutes. Each can draw the other into a wider world, a world in which both can flourish" (M13).

This sort of collaborative interaction lays heavy demands, then, on both sides. "Contemporary developments in science challenge theology far more deeply than did the introduction of Aristotle into Western Europe in the thirteenth century." (M12) Yet just as in the earlier case, this same challenge also promises resources for new development, but only if there are those who are capable of playing the role that Aquinas played long ago in rethinking the Aristotelian heritage within the Christian context. There will have to be theologians ". . . sufficiently well-versed in the sciences to make authentic and creative use of the resources the best-established theories may offer them. Such an expertise would prevent them from making uncritical and overhasty use for apologetic purposes of such recent theories as that of the 'Big Bang' in cosmology". (M 11-12)

The reference to recent discussions of the "anthropic principle" in cosmology is unmistakable. Several cosmologists in the mid-1970's suggested that the joint application of relativity theory and quantum theory to the first moments of formation of our universe, ten to twenty billion years ago, indicates that an extraordinary degree of "fine-tuning" would have been required in order to bring about a universe in which complex life could develop. Many saw in this a potential natural theology of the classical sort, where an omniscient Creator has to be invoked in order to account for some puzzling features of the universe that natural science has discovered but, in principle, cannot itself explain. Several of the papers at the Castel Gandolfo conference dealt with this topic; there seems to have been general agreement that, despite the apparent consonance between some aspects of early-universe cosmology and the Christian tradition of a "creation from nothing", reliance on current cosmology as a means of proving the existence of God would be not just premature, but straightforwardly impermissible. Pius XII was less cautious in his 1951 address; his invocation of cosmology in the service of theology, though carefully hedged, set off a fierce debate among cosmologists at the time.

At the height of the "creation-science" dispute in the U.S. some years ago, the National Academy of Sciences issued a declaration maintaining that religion and science are, in principle, entirely separate domains, one pertaining to faith and the other to reason, and hence of no possible relevance to one another. The new papal message takes issue with this convenient and popular way of avoiding the risks of conflict. The expertise that would prevent Christian thinkers from exaggerating the contributions of recent science would also keep them " . . . from discounting altogether the potential of such theories to the deepening of understanding in traditional areas of theological inquiry".(M12)

The illustrations that John Paul II chooses to make this point are quite striking:

> If the cosmologies of the ancient Near Eastern world could be purified and assimilated into the first chapters of Genesis, might contemporary cosmology have something to offer to our reflections on creation? Does our evolutionary perspective bring any light to bear on theological anthropology . . ., [on] the problem of Christology, and even upon the development of doctrine itself? What, if any, are the eschatological implications of contemporary cosmology, especially in light of the vast future of our universe? Can theological method fruitfully appropriate insights from . . . the philosophy of science? (M11)

What might startle Catholic theologians here is not so much the questions themselves as the fact that theologians are being challenged by the Pope to take them seriously. It is not so long since Teilhard de Chardin urged some of these same questions on theologians. Though Rome found

Teilhard's answers to them wanting, John Paul's letter makes it clear that the questions themselves must continue to be posed:

> Theology will have to call on the findings of science to one degree or another as it pursues its primary concern for the human person, the reaches of freedom, the possibilities of Christian community, the nature of belief and the intelligibility of nature and history. The vitality and significance of theology for humanity will in a profound way be reflected in its ability to incorporate those findings (M10).

Does this advice not run the risk of saddling theological doctrine with outmoded scientific formulations? If there is one thing that philosophers of science are agreed on today, it is the provisional character of scientific theory. When Einstein's mechanics superseded Newton's in the early part of this century, it became clear that even a theory with two centuries of predictive successes to its credit could one day be replaced. Suppose Catholic theologians were to take natural science seriously, as their predecessors did Aristotelian natural philosophy. Suppose they were to turn to evolutionary theory as a source of insight, for example, might their theology not become as provisional as the scientific theory it draws upon?

One of the most striking paragraphs in the Papal letter deals with just this issue, recognizing it to be an exceptionally delicate one. On the one hand, theologians obviously ought not try to incorporate every new theory as it appears. As the findings of science or of philosophy ". . . become part of the intellectual culture of the time, however, theologians must understand them and test their value in bringing out from Christian belief some of the possibilities which have not yet been realized" (M10). If they are found of value in this task, does this lend them something of the authority of the theological doctrine? During the revival of Thomism in the pontificates of Leo XIII and Pius X, one of the arguments used in support of Thomistic philosophy was that it had been employed in the formulation of defined dogma. The Council of Trent, for example, defined the doctrine of the Eucharist in terms of "transubstantiation", the substance of the bread being replaced by that of Christ. Did this not attach the authority of the Council to the Aristotelian distinction between substance and accident that the Council found so apt for its purposes? Some of the papal documents of a century ago certainly seemed to imply this.

The new papal message sets aside (once for all, one hopes) this supposed implication:

The hylomorphism of Aristotelian natural philosophy, for example, was adopted by medieval theologians to help them explore the nature of the sacraments and the hypostatic union. This did not mean that the Church adjudicated the truth or falsity of the Aristotelian insight, since that is not her concern. It did mean that this was one of the rich insights offered by Greek culture, that it needed to be understood and taken seriously and tested for its value in illuminating various areas of theology (M10-11).

The Church's competence does not extend to the determination of truth in domains other than theology. Theologians make use of the best insights of their own day, wherever they can find them. But whether these are scientific or philosophical, they are subject to challenge, to revision, even to replacement. At issue in the Galileo case long ago was the authority to be accorded to the common beliefs about nature embodied in the language of the Bible. It was not until 1893 that Leo XIII, in *Providentissimus Deus*, conceded the view for which Galileo had argued so eloquently, that the function of the Bible was not that of informing in matters scientific; the Biblical authors wrote for their own day, employing the images of nature they would have shared with their contemporaries.

It would scarcely have occurred to Leo XIII or to the other leaders of the Thomistic revival that a concession might also have to be made in regard to the use of philosophic categories in the formulation of theological dogmas. After all, natural philosophy was not, in their view, a matter of uncritical assumption, as was the Israelite belief in the reality of the daily motion of the sun. Rather, philosophy promised *demonstration*, as definitive in its own order, it would seem, as the declaration of dogma in theology.

Here, then, is an issue crucial in any discussion of how theology and the natural sciences should relate to one another. The Thomistic claim to a demonstrative philosophy of nature prior to, and thus in some sense normative of, modern experimental/theoretical science, finds little support today. It runs directly counter to much of the argument of philosophy of science in the last half-century. John Paul does not comment on this issue directly here. But what he does say is helpful in eliminating a major source of misunderstanding in past debates.

Theologians ,he suggests, draw upon the best that the philosophy and the science of their day have to offer. But this attaches no extra warrant to these other knowledge-claims. The implication in the Pope's assertion, that the Church in different ages will want to rethink its message in categories appropriate to each age, would surely raise a doubt as to whether the philosophic accomplishments of the medieval West can properly be regarded as normative for all later ages and places.

The central theme in the Papal letter is clearly stated. The human quest for understanding requires us to draw on a diversity of different sources. Science is not merely a means to technical control or to accurate prediction; religion is not just a matter of moral action or of private converse between the individual and God. Each contributes to our understanding of the complex world in which we are set; the quest for understanding is thus necessarily a collaborative one, in which the autonomy of the constituents must be respected. Within each there is an evident drive to unification. " The Church has entered into the movement for the union of all Christians . . . In reflection and prayer she has reached out to the great world-religions, recognizing the values we all hold in common and our universal and utter dependence on God" (M3). "Within the Church, herself, there is a growing sense of 'world-church,' so much in evidence at the last Ecumenical Council in which bishops native to every continent- no longer predominately of European or even Western origin- assumed for the first time their common responsibility for the entire Church." (M4)

Likewise in the natural sciences, we can discern analogies to this quest for unity, namely "the discovery of levels of law and process which unify created reality and which at the same time have given rise to the vast diversity of structures and organisms which constitute the physical and biological, and even the psychological and sociological, worlds" (M6). In physics, for example, the efforts to unify the four fundamental forces of nature in a single formalism have met with increasing success.

The relation between religion and science cannot, however, be a unity of the sort that each separately aspires to. The dialogue must be an open and honest one, in which each retains its autonomy:

> The unity that we seek . . . is not identity. The Church does not propose that science should become religion or religion science.   On the contrary, unity always presupposes the diversity and the integrity of its elements.   Each of these members should become not less itself but more itself in a dynamic interchange, for a unity in which one of the elements is reduced to the other is destructive, false in its promises of harmony, and ruinous of the integrity of its components . . . Christianity possesses the source of its justification within itself, and does not expect science to constitute its primary apologetic. Science must bear witness to its own worth. While each can and should support the other as distinct dimensions of a common human culture, neither ought to assume that it

forms a necessary premise for the other. The unprecedented opportunity we have today is for a common interactive relationship in which each discipline retains its integrity and yet is radically open to the discoveries and insights of the other (M8-9).

John Paul's letter proposes no solutions to the numerous specific problems where the competencies of Christian theology and of natural science appear to overlap. Its intent is simply to chart a very general course, and this it does in a refreshingly forthright way. It is candid about the past and optimistic about the future. It strikes, to my mind, exactly the right note, challenging as it does the theologian and the scientist alike. The relations of science and religion can never in the nature of things be entirely easy. But if they are approached with the honesty and humility that this document both recommends and exemplifies, there is hope that each can genuinely supplement the other.

SIGNS OF CONTRADICTION

Carl Mitcham

Certainly there is in this world . . . a considerable margin of
freedom for the Church's mission. But often it is no more
than a margin. One need only take note of the principal
tendencies governing the means of social communication [and]
pay heed to what is passed over in silence and what is shouted
aloud . . . to perceive that even where Christ is accepted there
is at the same time opposition to the full truth of his . . .
Gospel. There is a desire to . . . adapt him to suit . . . this ear
of progress and make him fit in with the program of modern
civilization – which is a program of consumerism and not of
transcendental ends. – Karol Wojtyla[1]

Pope John Paul II, in his open letter to the Reverend George V.
Coyne, S.J., on ". . . some issues which the interactions among natural
science, philosophy, and theology present to the Church and to human
society in general . . ."(M1-2), observes the existence of a new religion-
science dialogue. This new dialogue should, he argues, be continued, to the
benefit of both religion and science.

To pose a counter thesis to the Pope's message is difficult, since his
remarks seem so obviously fitting to the scientific age and because of an
inherent respect for the position he represents. Yet there is a possibility that
the message overlooks some fundamental issues at stake between religion
and science today, and misses an opportunity to deepen a theological analysis
of development adumbrated, for instance, in the encyclical *Sollicitudo rei
socialis*. In the space of a few words one can do no more than sketch the
basis of such a judgment.

It is appropriate to begin with brief commentaries on some specific
words of the text. Although the letter stresses that the dialogue to be
encouraged should not merge religion and science, there appear to be other
unstated parameters that would define the limits of the religion-science
encounter. Consider the following cases in point:

1. The letter begins by distinguishing the social institutions of Church
and Academy. The former refers, in the first instance, to the Catholic
Church, but also to all Christianity and, in the broadest sense, simply to
religion; the latter apparently includes all secular learning, although the
emphasis is clearly on modern natural science. Both are said to have ". . .
histories stretching back over thousands of years: the learned, academic
community dating back to the origins of culture, to the city and the library

and the school, and the Church with her historical roots in ancient Israel."
(M2)

This opening observation fails adequately to emphasize or even to
acknowledge the well-documented distinction between ancient and modern
science accepted by both pre- and post-Kuhnian historians and philosophers
of science, not to mention the originators of modern science themselves. It
thus appears to support the uncritical acceptance of that self-conception of
science that functions as a legitimating ideology in high school science
textbooks and popular opinion. In failing to acknowledge a fundamental
break between ancients and moderns in the field of natural science – and of
modern natural science from other fields of secular learning – there is thus
a failure to appreciate a basic imbalance between two social institutions.
Religion includes connections with premodern traditions of human
experience that simply are not present in modern science.

In noting the historical existence of various contacts between religion
and science, the letter further describes these as sometimes characterized by
". . . mutual support, at other times in those needless conflicts which have
marred both our histories" (M2). Is this meant to exclude the existence
either in the past or in the future of any necessary or salutary conflict?

2. By way of a second introductory observation, the letter claims that
in both religion and science centrifugal or separating forces are being
superceded by centripetal or unifying ones. Moreover, even between religion
and science there is a centripetal relationship, the beginning of a search for
areas of common ground. Both religion and science are universalizing and
unifying forces – presenting, respectively, a ". . . vision of the unity of all
things and all peoples in Christ" and ". . . an understanding and appreciation
of our universe as a whole . . . [including] animate and inanimate
components." (M5) Through modern technology, as well, modern science
provides concrete material unification in systems of transportation and
communication.

The idea that religion and science share a common ground surely
passes too lightly over the long warfare of science with theology in
Christendom, a century of reflection on differences between explanation in
the sciences and understanding in the *Geistwissenschaften*, and the crisis of
European sciences. The single most remarkable sentence in the text even
maintains that the Christian vision supports " . . . the values . . . emerging .
. . from our knowledge and appreciation of creation and of ourselves as the
products, knowers and stewards of creation." (M5) Not even the
circumlocutions of the Pontiff's prose can keep one from being startled by
the reference to human beings as "products" (a word with distinctly
technological connotations) of "creation," not to mention the idea that science

discourses on "creation" (rather than nature – and nature understood in a distinctly modern way).

The letter does mention in passing the persistence ". . . even within the academic community [of a] separation between truth and values. . ." that renders ". . . common discourse difficult if not at times impossible" (M2) – attributing to the arts and humanities as well the distinction between facts and values that has been a commonly promoted foundation for the sciences. As with the singular reference to technology as a handmaid of scientific unity, such a remark marginalizes what arguably should be an essential feature of any religion-science encounter.

The message here unnecessarily slights the concerns of many seriously religious individuals and communities regarding a spiritual uprootedness introduced into the heart of European culture by the abstractions and power of modern science, and of the contradictions inherent in scientific ideals. The struggle is not just ". . . to integrate the worlds of science and religion . . . [and to make] difficult moral decisions in matters of technological research and application" (M12), but to transform science – and to define and delimit a destructive unification in both its theory and practice. As Paul Ricoeur has summarized the situation:

> The phenomenon of universalization . . . constitutes a sort of subtle destruction, not only of traditional cultures . . . but also of the . . . creative nucleus of great civilizations and cultures . . . [I]n order to take part in modern civilization, it is necessary at the same time to take part in scientific, technical, and political rationality, something which very often requires the pure and simple abandon of a whole cultural past.[2]

3. In seeking to specify a positive role for science in theology the letter argues that theology must "test their [the sciences'] value in bringing out from Christian belief some of the possibilities which have not yet been realized." (M10) It neglects to emphasize that not all realizations are equally to be desired. Nor does it postulate the testing of science in terms of possibilities of Christian belief that might be obscured or even destroyed. Does this not slight a fundamental insight of the philosophy of history, that there is seldom if ever any simple unequivocal gain or progress? History is almost always ambiguous; whenever it reveals new possibilities it destroys old ones.

4. Finally, the letter argues that the time is right for more ". . . openness between the Church and the scientific communities . . ." (M7) as something mutually beneficial to both. For its part, the Church desires mutual understanding in which theologians are genuinely open to science and

scientists are genuinely open to religion. "Science can purify religion from
error and superstition; religion can purify science from idolatry and false
absolutes" (M13).

What remains unstated in such a call for mutual openness is that this
has been the appeal of progressive Christianity since the Enlightenment – but
that it is a stance which has proven impotent in the one aspect of most
significance to religion. Over and over again theologians in the West have
sought accommodation with modern science, admitting the need to relieve
Christianity of superstition, but also claiming the legitimate right of
Christianity to purify or supplement science. But although Christianity has
certainly been transformed – and it is unfair to say that this has consisted in
any unqualified removal of error and superstition – it is not clear that
Christianity has had any salutary impact on science, other than the well-
established historical one of providing some cultural basis for its genesis.
One is forced to ask whose real interest such a call serves, remembering that
no scientific institution has ever felt compelled to appeal for accommodation
with Christianity.

In light of these specific comments, more general observations may
perhaps be ventured. Although a discussion of science plays no serious role
in Karol Wojtyla's philosophical or theological work prior to his elevation to
the papacy,[3] since then the issue of science – and especially of the relation
between theology and science – has been a consistent minor theme of his
talks, particularly to academic audiences.[4] Indeed, the letter under discussion
exhibits a natural consistency with previous elocutions on this theme[5] – a
point that commentary has tended to overlook.[6]

Given the historical circumstances thus surrounding such statements,
one may reasonably postulate a certain prudence or diplomacy in their
character. Indeed, in one sense there is nothing at all remarkable or special
about this particular open letter to the editor of a set of proceedings from
a Vatican Observatory conference commemorating the 300th anniversary of
the publication of Newton's *Principia*.

The view articulated here and elsewhere by the Pope is, however,
quite remarkable – although not precisely in the way some commentators
have described. What is remarkable is its silence with regard both to a
tradition of critical spiritual reflection on science and to principles that the
Pope himself has clearly enunciated elsewhere. The fundamental issue is
two-fold. It concerns not only the pastoral appropriateness of the tactical
silences, but also the theoretical adequacy of a principled distinction in which
they are grounded.

What the letter presents is a theoretical-realist interpretation of science and a doctrinal-realist view of revelation and religion. The truth is that such a position depends on a highly controversial view of science itself[7] and is heavily tipped toward abstract theoretical issues, on the ground that scientific theory can be separated from applied scientific practice and scientific culture.

In the present letter there is only passing allusion to how "the uses of science have on more than one occasion proven massively destructive . . ." (M14), but even the most cursory reading of *L'Osservatore Romano, The Pope Speaks,* or *Origins* would reveal that the Pontiff more regularly addresses issues of the relation between religion and applied science or technology than between religion and pure science.[8] The general theme of all such pronouncements is the need for what Henri Bergson first called a "supplement of soul".[9]

It is also the case that the Pope recognizes the dangers of what he calls "scientific mentality" and "scientism" – what might also be called the "modern scientific spirit" – as fundamentally opposed to religion.[10] At the same time, in his remarks on pure or theoretical science he wants to maintain that there is no inherent opposition – although there exists "a moral duty [for scientists] to carry out their activities at the service of humanity".[11] The ultimate questions concern whether the rigid pure science-applied science distinction can either hold up on its own or serve as adequate basis for spiritual guidance (although it certainly functions well as ideological legitimation), and how the criteria of service to humanity is to be exercised.

The purpose in this questioning, it should be emphasized, is not to reject the legitimacy of scientific and doctrinal realism as contributions to the religion-science encounter, nor to impugn the sincerity of Christian scientists and others who would promote this approach. It is only to argue that such views are part – and must be seen as only a part – of a much larger spectrum in both philosophical and theological reflections on science. Normally it would be recognized among both philosophical and theological interpreters of science that the realist view of religion-science complementarity needs to be and has been supplemented by others, and that any religion-science dialogue that wholly excludes the concerns of what may be called the existential-spiritual critique of modern natural science is woefully inadequate.[12] The letter alludes to a "movement towards the kind of unity which resists homogenization and relishes diversity" (M3), but in its own terms does not exhibit sufficient commitment to diversity.

Within a principled commitment to a legitimate role for the Pope's position in any truly pluralistic religion-science dialogue, one can nevertheless question its adequacy. Whether it is most accurate to speak of science as what some phenomenologists have called a "regionalized ontology" or,

instead, as a way of being-in-the-world, that is, a way of life, is surely an issue
to be considered.   In the latter case, on the basis of less doctrinaire
separation between pure and applied science, one can readily suggest that it
is time to call even pure scientists to responsibility for their excessive
projects.   For the reality is that modern science is no longer, if it ever was,
simply a disinterested search for truth. As Simone Weil once observed, and
as has been fully confirmed by recent literature in the sociology of science:

> . . . the acquisition of fresh knowledge is not a sufficient
> stimulant to encourage scientists in their efforts.   Other
> stimulants are needed. To start with, they have the stimulant
> which is found in the chase, in sport, in a game.   One often
> hears mathematicians comparing their specialty to a game of
> chess.[13]

Beyond games and striving for prestige, bureaucratized transnational
science is today caught up in the political promotion of gigantic funding
programs that inevitably compete for money that could be otherwise spent
to promote social or distributive justice.   There is a politics as well as a
theory of pure science.[14]

Contemporary science thus partakes in the "superdevelopment" that
the Pope denounces in his encyclical *Sollicitudo rei socialis*. As the Pope
clearly says:

> . . . the mere accumulation of goods and services, even for the
> benefit of the majority, is not enough for the realization of
> human happiness.   Nor, in consequence, does the availability
> of the many real benefits provided in recent times by science
> and technology, including the computer sciences, bring
> freedom from every form of slavery.[15]

Among the contemporary forms of idolatry, *Sollicitudo rei socialis*
mentions not just money, ideology, and class, but also technology. Each such
idolatry partakes in and manifests "structures of sin". But surely what Derek
DeSolla Price has so simply and accurately called "big science" – the
theoretical physics that demands $8 billion for a superconducting
supercollider, or the theoretical biology that would appropriate $5 billion for
the Human Genome Project – a science that is constantly returning to the
trough of public and private funding, publicly justifying itself in terms of its
consumer product spinoffs, is part of the modern world of consumerism and
exhibits its own sinful social structures. The growing problem of fraud in
science is no small testimony to this phenomenon.[16]

There is, one may even suggest, a consumerist mentality that can be manifest in the search for ever increasing amounts of information and knowledge. St. Bernard refers to the need to exercise asceticism even in the cognitive life, guarding against *curiositas*[17], and even August Comte speaks of a need to exercise a hygiene of the mind as well as of the body. As with food or sexual pleasure, simply because knowledge itself is good does not mean that it can be pursued without limit. In its desire for ever more knowledge, it is not at all clear that modern science has not lost hold of that general ascesis from which it sprang as a specialized methodology.

On other occasions John Paul II has spoken of Christ as a sign of contradiction. By choosing, in the present letter, not to contradict certain self-images of science, there one may sense a certain contradiction of that very contradiction – and a missed opportunity to encourage many to live their most fundamental commitments, and an unwitting contribution to narrowing the margins for Christianity in the modern world beyond those otherwise present.

Notes

1. Karol Wojtyla, *Sign of Contradiction* (New York: Seabury, 1979) 199.

2. Paul Ricoeur, "Universal Civilization and National Cultures," in *History and Truth*, trans. Charles A. Kelbley (Evanston, IL: Northwestern University Press, 1965) 271. See also Jean Ladriere, *The Challenge Presented to Cultures by Science and Technology* (Paris: United Nations Educational, Scientific and Cultural Organization, 1977).

3. Both science and technology are, for instance, conspicuous by their absence in Karol Wojtyla, *The Acting Person*, trans. Andrezej Potocki, *Analecta Husserliana* 10 (Boston: D. Reidel, 1979 [Polish original 1969]).

4. On the basis of the Pope's own references on other occasions, there are at least five key talks on this theme: at the Institute Catholique, Paris (1 June 1980); at UNESCO, Paris (2 June 1980); at the Cologne Cathedral (15 November 1980); at the UN Hiroshima University (25 February 1981); and at CERN (15 June 1982). But see also the five "Addresses About Science and Faith" collected in *The Whole Truth About Man: John Paul II to University Faculties and Students,* ed. James V. Schall (Boston: Daughters of St. Paul, 1981) 159-205.

5. See, for instance, "Science and the Church in the Nuclear Age," at the European Center for Nuclear Research (CERN), 15 June 1982, which proposes the existence of a new religion-science dialogue, says it should continue, and affirms the complementary non-identity of religion and science.

6. See, e.g., Ernan McMullin, "A Common Quest for Understanding," *America* 160 (11 February 1989) 100-104. According to McMullin "Pope John Paul II's recent declaration on the relations of science and religion may well be the most important Roman statement on this

topic since Pius XII's address to the Pontifical Academy of Science in 1951" (p. 100). Reprinted in this volume.

7. The unacceptable implications of both positions to most scientists would have been more obvious had the letter included any references to the social sciences. According to John Paul II, history, sociology, psychology, anthropology, etc. must simply accept the datum of revelation as a given in their scientific fields. See George Huntston Williams, *The Mind of John Paul II: Origins of His Thought and Action* (New York: Seabury, 1981) 347.

8. For instance, between 1978 (the first year of the pontificate of John Paul II) and 1988, *The Pope Speaks* prints at least twenty talks on applied science and technology (nuclear energy, euthanasia, biological experimentation, medical ethics, ecology, etc. -- not including numerous others on contraception, art, agriculture, the communications media, and the problems of labor) but only five on pure science.

9. Henri Bergson, *Les deux sources de la morale et de la religion* (Paris: Alcan, 1932). This idea is already present in *Redemptor hominis*, where John Paul II writes that "The progress of technology and of a contemporary civilization that is characterized by the primacy of the technical calls for a comparable development of the moral life and ethical discipline. This latter development, unfortunately, seems always to lag behind" (no. 15). See also, e.g., "Dialogue with Post-Modern Society," *Pope Speaks* 33, no. 3 (Fall 1988) 194: The Church "is taking pains to give a soul to cultural changes in the domain of thought, artistic creation, and scientific research."

10. See, e.g., "Science and Unbelief," *Pope Speaks* 26, no. 3 (Fall 1981) 209-213.

11. "Science and Progress," *Pope Speaks* 27, no. 4 (Winter 1982) 366. "Today more than ever, science must *contribute with all its power to true human progress* and it must banish the real threat of the criminal uses of its discoveries" (p. 368). Note, too, that the Pontifical Academy of Sciences was founded to promote not just a religion-science dialogue but science in the service of the Church.

12. For a much more inclusive spectrum of positions in a religion-science dialogue, see David Ray Griffin, William A. Beardslee, and Joe Holland, *Varieties of Postmodern Theology* (Albany: State University of New York Press, 1989), which includes an interpretation of the views of John Paul II.

13. Simone Weil, *The Need for Roots* (New York: Putnam, 1951) 254.

14. See, e.g., Daniel S. Greenberg, *The Politics of Pure Science* (New York: New American Library, 1967); and David Dickson, *The New Politics of Science* (Chicago: University of Chicago Press, 1984).

15. *Sollicitudo rei socialis*, no. 28.

16. See, e.g., William Broad and Nicholas Wade, *Betrayers of the Truth* (New York: Simon and Schuster, 1982).

17. Bernard of Clairvaux, *De gradibus humilitatis* X. For a careful study (and defense) of the modern habilitation paralleling that associated with selfishness in economics see Hans Blumenberg, *The Legitimacy of the Modern Age*, trans. Robert M. Wallace (Cambridge, MA: MIT Press, 1983) Part III, "The 'Trial' of Theoretical Curiosity."

THE MESSAGE OF POPE JOHN PAUL II ON SCIENCE
AND THE CHURCH: A RESPONSE

Nancey Murphy

Introduction

The papal message on science and the Church has a number of features that deserve commendation. One of its most valuable aspects is the historical perspective it brings to the current discussion. It compares the benefits to be gained if contemporary theology would more adequately reflect its scientific milieu to those gained from the use of Aristotelian thought in the Thomistic synthesis and from the assimilation of ancient Near Eastern cosmologies into the first chapters of Genesis.

I wish to call special attention to the paragraph on page M 11; here appear some sample areas where the ". . . vitality and significance of theology for humanity . . ." (M 10) might be profoundly enhanced by incorporating into theology the findings of science and philosophy. Other authors will be able to comment more competently than I on the revitalizing potentials of current cosmology and evolutionary biology. I intend to explore instead the suggestion that theology might benefit from insights drawn from scientific methodology and philosophy of science. From such a brief statement it is not possible to say exactly what is intended here. My response to the message, then, will not first of all be to analyze and criticize what has been said, but rather to attempt to explore this avenue for dialogue between theology and science. I shall offer what I take to be the strongest possible reading that does not conflict with the rest of the document. I hope to show that theology can borrow *significantly* from scientific methodology without violating the cautions that the document raises regarding the identity and autonomy of the disciplines. Thus I first explore how theological method might be conceived in light of recent philosophy of science; then I consider whether this proposal is consistent with the Pope's view of unification in diversity.

The importance of showing the science-like character of theology cannot be overemphasized. The meaning of *scientia* has changed since medieval times, when theology was established as the queen of the sciences. The failure of theology to adapt to this change has led to serious questioning of the rational credibility of theology.[1] Without the adoption of a scientism that claims that only the sciences provide knowledge, it is still possible to claim that our everyday understanding of how we reason from experience has been changed by the rise of modern science. So long as it is not shown that knowledge of things religious conforms to that understanding, theology will have to justify its anomalous character. The history of modern philosophical theology is by and large a history of rather unconvincing attempts to do just that. If it can be shown that theology is (once again, in these new circumstances) at least potentially scientific, then this apologetic problem is solved. Furthermore, philosophy of science can then serve as a useful guide for evaluating theological proposals.

Philosophy of Science and Theological Method

Let us begin with our everyday understanding of the nature of reasoning from experience. Consider the description provided in the papal document:

> When human beings seek to understand the multiplicities that surround them, when they seek to make sense of experience, they do so by bringing many factors into a common vision. Understanding is achieved when many data are unified by a common structure. The one illuminates the many; it makes sense of the whole. Simple multiplicity is chaos; an insight, a single model, can give that chaos structure and draw it into intelligibility. (M9)

This account might be a description of sense perception – the recognition of a unified object in a multiplicity of chaotic sense impressions – or the recognition of a personality trait that unifies a multiplicity of individual actions, or whatever. However, it could also have been written by philosopher of science Stephen Toulmin as a description of scientific reasoning.[2] And does it not apply equally well to reasoning in religious matters? For example, we might describe the disciples' struggle in the Gospels to say who Jesus was (for example, the son of David, Son of Man, Messiah) as a struggle to unify their chaotic impressions of his ministry and his person. Let me nuance this account of reasoning by presenting a brief summary of the conclusions of philosophers of science. Then we shall see how well it applies to reasoning in theology.

The basic form of reasoning in science has been called "the way up and down" by J.S. Mill, or "abduction" by C.S. Peirce, or more recently, "hypothetico-deductive reasoning" by Carl Hempel. The data from observation or experiment support more general scientific conclusions not because one can reason from them to the conclusions, either inductively or deductively, but rather because one can reason from the conclusions (backwards) to the data. Hempel claimed that in science one forms a hypothesis which, if true, would explain a set of data. However, since more than one hypothesis can always be invented to explain a given set of data, one must then go on to test the hypothesis by drawing further consequences from it and seeing whether they are borne out by experiment or observation.

So we are justified in accepting a conclusion if, in the language of the papal message, it unifies, illuminates, and makes sense of a multiplicity of data. But Hempel would warn us that this account of reasoning needs to be amended, since alternative explanations are always possible, so the hallmark of science (and of good reasoning in general) is the careful testing of one's conclusions against further experience.

During the past generation Hempel's own model of scientific reasoning has been amplified in at least three ways. First, it has been noted that all scientific facts are theory-laden. There are no facts free of interpretation. As the papal message recognizes, unstructured observations are simply a chaos, so scientific theories are needed to give meaning to observations. Thus there is a measure of circularity in using theory-impregnated data to support theories.

Second, testing in science is always, in fact, the testing of a whole network of theories at once. Theories are logically related not only to their data but to one another, and no abstract theory standing alone will ever have empirical consequences.

Third, since alternative explanations of data are possible, and because there can never be any definitive verification or falsification of a theory, tests in science are usually attempts to assess the relative degree of support for two or more competing networks of theories.

More recent accounts of science, beginning with Thomas Kuhn, therefore, emphasize revolutions, where one paradigm (network of theory, appropriate body of data, exemplary methods of research, standards for problem solution) replaces its competitor.[3] Or one may employ the theories of Imre Lakatos to speak instead of one research program (core theory, auxiliary hypotheses, plan for developing the program, and appropriate data) being judged more progressive than its rivals (i.e., being able to account for more new facts without having to resort to *ad hoc* theoretical adjustments).[4]

Now, if the simplified account of reasoning with which we began applies to ordinary reasoning in religious matters (as well as in science), perhaps this more sophisticated account from recent philosophy of science will apply to the more sophisticated reasoning of theologians.[5] For example, consider Augustine's doctrine of original sin. Can we fruitfully compare it to a scientific theory?

Augustine was much preoccupied throughout his life by the problem of evil – evil done and evil suffered. Whence did it come? He was aware of competing theories. For example, there was the Manichaean view that the universe was controlled by rival deities: a wholly good but passive god under constant attack by an equally powerful but aggressive evil force. But this theory was incompatible with some of the data from Scripture, where God is represented as being not only wholly good, but also active and powerful. Only some dreadful sin, Augustine hypothesized, could account for God's sending the human race such terrible affliction; in Adam's sin the whole race had fallen and present suffering was (partially) explicable as punishment for that first sin.

This theory of original sin is an instructive example to raise here, since we can clearly see in it the important role played by Augustine's culture. The idea that some great sin lay behind the misery of the human condition was shared by Christians and pagans alike in late antiquity.[6] So in this sense Augustine's theory was not a truly novel explanation of human suffering. He went on, however, to explain the continuing sinfulness of the human race: the first sin disordered human capacities, damaging the will and redirecting the emotions. He also accounted for the *universality* of sin and suffering by postulating the sexual transmission of the sin, and found at least symbolic confirmation of this in Scripture in the fact that Adam and Eve were said to have covered their genitals after their disobedience – the aprons were a clue to the locus of the problem. He eventually worked the theory of original sin into a complex network of theories – including his doctrine of God, theory of atonement, and a complete theological anthropology – and defended the network against competitors such as Pelagius. The Pelagian theory, Augustine claimed, was unable to account for the complexity of human motivation.[7]

So here we have a theory that was proposed to account for observed facts, could be checked against other confirming data from Scripture and experience, and was related to a network of other theories. All of this is exactly in accord with a (simplified) model of scientific reasoning.

If we consider theological doctrines to be theories constructed to explain the data from Scripture and experience, two sorts of consequences follow. First, all the careful work by philosophers of science on the question of how to choose among competing scientific theories will be available to theologians for evaluating their proposals.[8]

Second, two roles for the use of the *content* of science in theology become apparent: (a) Scientific research provides a growing body of phenomena to serve as data for theological theories. For example, if Augustine's goal was to account for the evil in human behavior, conclusions from psychology, biology, and anthropology – both as descriptions of behavior and as attempts to account for it – might be useful today in approaching that same problem; (b) Since scientific theories are hypotheses – human inventions – the concepts used in their formulation have to be drawn from available (cultural) resources. So just as Augustine borrowed an idea from his culture – a primordial Fall – contemporary theologians will inevitably borrow ideas from their own cultures, including science. As the papal message suggests, evolutionary theories might be one important cultural resource for a revitalized theological anthropology.

Unification in Diversity

The unifying theme of the papal message is unity. The new impetus toward the unification of the cultures of science and the Church that it encourages is set within the context of the drive toward unity among the religions of the world and within science itself – and all is interpreted as a response to the desire of Christ that all might be one. However, the message is careful to stress the separate identities of science and religion, and to note that their working toward increased cooperation and understanding presupposes these separate identities. It would indeed be a step backwards to lose sight of the hard-won differentiation between science on the one hand and religion or theology on the other. Therefore, I dedicate the following paragraphs to a review of the document's cautions in this area, seeing what they might mean for the specific area of dialogue addressed above, namely, the borrowing for theology of methodology from science.

The message cautions that science should not become religion nor religion science. Each must preserve its autonomy and distinctiveness, possessing its own principles, patterns and procedures, diversities of interpretation, and conclusions. Neither discipline is founded on the other; Christianity in particular possesses the source of its justification within itself and does not expect science to constitute its primary apologetic (M 8-9). Finally, theology is not to incorporate indifferently each new scientific or philosophical theory; each must be tested for its value in bringing out unrealized possibilities for Christian belief (M 10-11).

The value of significant borrowing by philosophical theologians from the philosophy of science can only be fully known by experiment. Does an understanding of theological methodology based on parallels with science cast new light on the theological task? Does it give direction for constructive theology and for assessing the relative merits of competing theological proposals? I predict that the answers to these questions will be yes.

But the question must also be raised whether such a borrowing of methodological standards would destroy the distinctiveness and autonomy of theology. Here I recall Bernard Lonergan's claim that there are patterns in human cognition regardless of the subject matter under consideration.[9] If we take theology to be a rational enterprise at all,[10] then, following Lonergan, we must suppose that at a deep level there will necessarily be commonalities between science and theology. Yet a common structure or pattern of reasoning (whether it is best described by Lonergan or, as I would suggest, by recent philosophers of science) does not detract from the distinctiveness or autonomy of the various disciplines. We may distinguish here between *methodology*, which is an abstract, overarching theory of justification, and *methods*, which are the concrete research and experimental procedures proper to each discipline. The pattern of reasoning in justifying a theory may be the same in biology and physics, in systematic theology and biblical exegesis, but the biologist, the physicist, the theologian, and the exegete will still necessarily use different research methods.

Each turns, as well, to a distinctive range or domain of data, despite the fact that there may be some degree of overlap of the domains.[11] So, for example, although findings regarding human behavior will be as relevant to a theological anthropology as to a psychological account of the human person, the primary data for a Christian anthropology will still be found within the Christian tradition. And, as Lonergan has pointed out, the conclusions of one discipline may serve as data for another. The conclusions of exegete and cosmologist alike might serve as data for the theologian.

On the model proposed here, Christian theology would still possess the source of its justification within itself. The justification of any theory is a function of the relation it bears to its evidence and to other relevant theories. In this case, the data – the givens – could still be those traditional norms of Christian thought: the apostolic witness and the *consensus fidelium* (however these are understood within the relevant communion).

Conclusion

Much more space would be required to treat these issues adequately, but I hope at least to have suggested that theology could rely heavily on current canons of scientific reasoning without losing either its identity or its autonomy. I predict that doing so will have important consequences for theology. Just as human understanding of the natural world changes and develops through the centuries, so too does our understanding of human reasoning itself. Current philosophy of science has made extremely important contributions in this area. This being the case, theologians can learn to do better what they are already doing by considering their work in light of these new theories about theorizing. Furthermore, the ability to describe theological reasoning in terms accessible to those in the scientific culture will certainly enhance the possibilities for dialogue between science and the Church, and may even promote acceptance of the conclusions of theologians.[12]

Notes

1. See Wolfhart Pannenberg, *Theology and the Philosophy of Science* (Philadelphia: Westminster Press, 1976) 13, 20; and Jeffrey Stout, *The Flight from Authority* (Notre Dame: University of Notre Dame Press, 1981) ch. 2.

2. See Stephen Toulmin, *Foresight and Understanding* (New York: Harper, 1961).

3. Thomas Kuhn, *The Structure of Scientific Revolutions*, 2nd. ed. (Chicago: University of Chicago Press, 1970).

4. Imre Lakatos, "Falsification and the Methodology of Scientific Research Programmes," in *Criticism and the Growth of Knowledge*, eds. I. Lakatos and A. Musgrave (Cambridge: Cambridge University Press, 1970) 91-196. Reprinted as ch. 1 of *The Methodology of Scientific Research Programmes: Philosophical Papers, Volume One* (Cambridge: Cambridge University Press, 1978).

5. I have in fact argued this in detail elsewhere. See my *Theology in the Age of Scientific Reasoning* (Ithaca, NY: Cornell University Press, 1990).

6. See for example Peter Brown, *Augustine of Hippo* (Berkeley: University of California Press, 1967) 388.

7. *Ibid.*, p. 371.

8. I would especially recommend Lakatos's criteria. See his "Falsification and the Methodology of Scientific Research Programmes," *op. cit.*, see note 4.

9. See Bernard Lonergan,S.J., *Insight* (New York: Philosophical Library, 1958); and *Method in Theology* (New York: Seabury, 1972).

10. To my knowledge this has never been questioned in the Catholic tradition, but some Protestant theologians in the modern period have at least come close to denying it.

11. In cases of overlap, different interpretations of the same observations might be quite legitimate, due to different "auxiliary hypotheses" of a methodological nature within the different disciplines. Theology has long been struggling with the question whether the theologian's principles of interpretation of historical data must be the same as those of the secular historian. A cogent argument could be made, based on recent philosophy of science, that they need not be.

12. In light of the Catholic Church's renewed openness to the scientific culture, expressed in the words of Pope John Paul II, it may be time to reassess the works of the Catholic modernists. I believe that some of these writers (George Tyrell, especially) were attempting to do just what I have taken this document to recommend – namely, to reevaluate the nature of theology in light of scientific methodology and scientific conclusions, and thereby to provide a revitalized apologetic for traditional Catholic teaching. There is evidence that the condemnation of modernism was based on an attempt to fit their work into the deductive model of "conclusions theology" – a confusion of the modern concept of science with an Aristotelian concept of *scientia*. See Alec Vidler, *The Modernist Movement in the Roman Church* (Cambridge: Cambridge University Press, 1934) xii.

THEOLOGY AND PHILOSOPHY IN INTERACTION WITH SCIENCE: A RESPONSE TO THE MESSAGE OF POPE JOHN PAUL II ON THE OCCASION OF THE NEWTON TRICENTENNIAL IN 1987

Wolfhart Pannenberg

The message of Pope John Paul II encourages and even urges the need for dialogue between theology and science. A "self-imposed isolation" (M7) of theology over against science, as it was recommended in Protestant theology by Karl Barth and in his school, is – as the Pope says – "no longer acceptable," because "peoples cannot continue to live in separate compartments" (M8) regarding their relations to the world of nature. However, if neutrality on the part of the theologian, who after all has to interpret this same world as God's creation, is no longer justifiable, if it ever was, neither is identification with science. The Pope rightfully emphasizes the "autonomy" and "distinctiveness" of both, science and religion, and the same applies to theology and science. Neither is "a necessary premise for the other." Each indeed possesses "its own principles, its pattern of procedures, its diversities of interpretations and its own conclusions" (M8-9). Nevertheless, their mutual autonomy is not symmetrical. On the part of science, there is no dependence on theology, except perhaps for the metaphysical (or religious) inspirations that significantly contributed to the history of scientific terminology and were often effective in the guiding visions that underlie the work of creative scientists, as in the case of Einstein and Spinoza's metaphysics. The deep influence of such a guiding vision must not be underestimated, though there is not a dependence on the level of scientific argument. Theology, on the other hand, has to "incorporate" scientific "findings," as the Pope says. Its "ability" to do so indicates its "vitality and significance...for humanity" (M10). In other words, scientific "findings" belong among the evidence that theology must explain on its own level of interpretation, which is different from that of science. This is especially true in the doctrine of creation. But if there is a convergence between the evolutionary outlook in science and the concept of a divine economy of salvation, as the Pope suggests and as it has been asserted in British theology of evolution for more than a century, then the entire theological doctrine on the economy of God's action *ad extra* is affected. Thus, it is true of theology, not of science, that it must relate itself to the other, if the world interpreted theologically as God's creation is the same world that is described by science. Theological description of this world as God's creation presupposes that the world of nature admits of another description and interpretation beyond that of science. If the scientific description were exhaustive, a theological doctrine of creation would be either superfluous or at best a popular intimation of what is more precisely described by science.

On its own level of description science does not need, and does not even admit of, any other source to make it complete. That level as such, however, is characterized by a high degree of abstraction from the complexity of concrete natural processes, and it is at least open to debate whether that complexity can in the end be exhaustively absorbed by its reconstruction on the level of scientific description. This is a philosophical question that cannot itself be solved on the level of scientific demonstration and evidence. At this point, if not before, philosophy comes into the picture as a third partner in the dialogue between theology and science. Only by philosophical reflection can the different levels of argument be distinguished and interrelated as would, according to the words of the Pope, characterize theology and science in their mutual autonomy.

For this reason, modern science cannot simply take the place that Aristotelian philosophy occupied in relation to medieval theology, as the Pope at one point seems to suggest. One may even doubt that modern science can fully replace Aristotelian physics, not to speak of metaphysics and logic. Modern physics does not fully replace Aristotelian physics, if alongside science and theology a philosophy of nature (not only of scientific method) remains a possibility. The theologians, of course, may be their own philosophers, as many of the great medieval Patristic theologians were, in making "authentic and creative use" of Platonic or Aristotelian philosophy by adapting it to the special purposes of Christian theology: if such adaptation is done not by mere decree of the theologian, but as a result of argument on the level of philosophical reflection, then here the theologian functions as a philosopher.

Furthermore, philosophy is involved in accounting for the unity that connects and comprises the different levels of thought. At this point, the notion of "interactive relationship" (M9) is not enough to describe the relation between science and theology, if the relationship is not to be conceived as accidental, but is essential, at least in the work of theology. This seems to be the intention of the Pope in speaking of a "relational unity between science and religion" (M10). But then, that unity has to be understood as constitutive of the interrelationship itself. This actually seems to be implied when the Pope speaks of a "common structure" of meaning that comprehends the interactive relationship between science and religion. To ask for the creation of a framework of unified understanding that connects the different levels of scientific and theological thought surpasses significantly the somewhat vague talk of mere "consonance" between science and theology. The image of "consonance" remains vague, because consonance presupposes some unity in the midst of diversity, without however identifying that unity as such. A unified understanding, however, must reconstruct, however tentatively, a comprehensive unity, where, as the Pope says, "the one illuminates the many" when "many factors" are brought "into a common vision" (M9). The Pope explicitly says that within such a framework of unified understanding science and religion can each "support the other," without either becoming "a necessary premise for the other" (M9). I take this to mean that their unity does not become apparent on the methodological level of either science or theology, except for a theology that argues not only from revelation, but also moves on the level of philosophical reflection and argument. The unified "common structure" (M9) that the Pope envisions as comprehending scientific and religious thought will most appropriately be identified on a level of philosophical reflection discernible from both science and revealed religion, but not completely separated from theology, insofar as theology explicates the content of revealed faith by means of philosophical reflection.

In dealing with the concept of nature, philosophy and theology are analogously related to the sciences. A philosophy of nature must refer to scientific methods and findings as evidence for its own framework of interpretation, in a manner similar to theology as it interprets the world of nature as God's creation. In aiming at a comprehensive and coherent account for the world of human experience, as well as for the nature of such experience itself, philosophy may or may not use the notion of God, while theology aims at such a comprehensive account in terms of God, the God of revelation, as unifying source and destiny of all finite reality. In following through its own scheme of interpretation, theology will be critical of every nontheistic philosophical synthesis, and such criticism will have rational value only to the degree to which it appeals to criteria of consistency and coherence, the kind of criteria that also guide a philosophical critique of theological conceptions and assertions.

Theology as well as philosophy, then, has to take account of scientific "findings" and methodology when talking about the world of nature. Theology must try "to incorporate these findings" (M10) in its doctrine of the creation of the world. There indeed should be some analogy to the way ancient Near Eastern cosmologies were "purified and assimilated into the first chapters of Genesis" (M11) In the contemporary situation, however, the purification will not relate to scientific assertions and theories as such, because these are to be judged on the basis of empirical evidence. Theology cannot demand purification of assertions or theories that are in accordance with empirical fact. The long struggles over the Copernican cosmology or, more recently, over the theory of evolution, are cases in point. It is in the interpretation of scientific assertions, rather, where critical evaluation from a theological point of view can have a legitimacy.

What is undoubtedly true in science cannot be wrong in theology. But it is not always clear what should be acknowledged as indisputable empirical fact in science and what may be considered speculative extrapolation or at least as a more or less one-sided approximation of the true nature of reality. Here a degree of tension between dominating trends in scientific theory and the theological vision of the world as God's creation on its way towards its eschatological transfiguration may occur. The theologian must not be too quick to adapt theological ideas and language to the latest outlook in the sciences, especially where such adaption requires substantial readjustments of traditional doctrine. The theological vision of the world can also function as a challenge to science and as a source of inspiration in developing new strategies of research.

As modern science has been in continuous development and will go on to change in the foreseeable future, the theological vision of the world may be vindicated by future developments in science at points where tensions presently occur. On the other hand, theological doctrine as formulated in the past may have been overly dependent on assumptions of a timebound character, and, therefore, the effort at distinguishing the core of revealed truth in the doctrinal heritage from passing forms of its historical expression requires repeated renewal.

An example of the possible future vindication of theological vision may be the apparent convergence between contemporary scientific cosmology and the Christian affirmation of a beginning of this universe in God's creation. For centuries such a convergence was hardly conceivable. It now becomes apparent that Christian theology was well advised not to give up on the connection of the doctrine of creation to the notion of a beginning of the universe, though in terms not of a beginning in time, but rather of time itself. It is no longer inconceivable that a similar convergence could emerge between scientific cosmology and the eschatological affirmations of the Christian faith concerning the future of this world. Still the papal address very wisely warns against ". . . uncritical and overhasty use for apologetic purposes of such recent theories as that of the 'Big Bang' in cosmology" (M11-12). The notorious fluidity in the process of scientific discussions, especially in the field of cosmological models, should alert the theologian to those aspects of the theories under discussion that prevent claims to complete agreement between science and theology. The creation of the world continues to be a theological affirmation that is not completely identical with any result of scientific theory. But neither is there incompatibility. To the contrary, in the present situation there is a remarkable degree of convergence.

An example of the need for readjustment of theological vision, the need for theology to reassess doctrinal affirmations of the past in the light of modern scientific developments, seems to be presented by the theory of evolution of life. Certain continuing difficulties of evolutionary theory notwithstanding, theology should be open to a reinterpretation of its anthropological doctrines in the light of some combination of evolutionism and salvation history as advocated by British theologians for more than a century, as well as by Catholic theologians such as Teilhard de Chardin and Karl Rahner. Such a reinterpretation would require us to consider whether assumptions such as monogenism as an historical belief need not be essential to a Christian account of human nature and destiny. The papal address sounds remarkably open with regard to the bearing of an ". . . evolutionary perspective . . . upon theological anthropology" (M11). Although the issue of monogenism is not explicitly mentioned, it goes by implication that an evolutionary perspective would require a great deal of reinterpretation of the traditional teachings on anthropology, not least with respect to the doctrine of original sin. It is in this area that a new effort is especially urgent, one distinguishing the perennial core of the traditional doctrine from historical conditions of its formulation, which cannot claim permanent validity. It is important that the papal address does not preclude further discussion on these issues but rather encourages the theological exploration of new solutions.

COMMENTS ON "THE CHURCH AND THE SCIENTIFIC COMMUNITIES: A COMMON QUEST FOR UNDERSTANDING" BY HIS HOLINESS JOHN PAUL II

Tullio Regge

Since their ancient beginnings great religions and science have been at odds and have engaged in furious and passionate polemics. The blot left on our mutual history by the trial of Galileo has not yet been erased, and there are still fanatics who wish to revive the monkey trials. In turn there is widespread scorn of religious beliefs in the scientific community. Can we avoid these conflicts; can we heal the wounds of the past? Is the practice of religion compatible with scientific research?

In view of the many noted scientists throughout the world who are deeply religious, the answer should be in the affirmative. Mere coexistence of science and belief is, however, not enough for the Pontiff, and his very elaborate introduction makes thoughtful and carefully balanced ideological statements on the relationship between science and religion. The document is important; it clearly addresses all scientists, not only Catholics, and should be read carefully by everyone interested in these matters.

The Pontiff wants more than good manners. He sees science more as a peculiar kind of religion and less as the heterogenous society of fellow scientists which I perceive it to be. Nevertheless, the papal document is a tentative and prudent opening toward the scientific world at large; it is an open invitation for a lively exchange of ideas.

I feel that the road to final understanding and unification of science and religion is a very long and perilous one, and at the moment, I am satisfied simply with harmonious coexistence. Personally, I would have felt relieved if the Pontiff had discussed in more detail what he calls the "needless conflicts" of the past between science and religion. This could have been a good opportunity to discuss Galileo's trial and to state clearly where the Church stands now.

The last pages of the document are intense, reflective and structured into mutually balancing statements. The Pontiff recalls and marvels at the medieval synthesis of the Aristotelian hylomorphism and theology and wonders if any future theologian could assimilate contemporary cosmology into religious beliefs, a most startling proposal. His phrasing is subtle and the implications not always obvious on a first reading.

He states that the Church does not adjudicate the truth or falsity of Aristotelian insight, since, in his words, "that is not her concern" (M11). Quite clearly he implies the same attitude toward contemporary science, and with it toward the Big Bang model and the theory of evolution, a subject of hot controversy. In this he departs radically from the past. I certainly agree with him on this point. I could add that religious beliefs are not the concern of science either.

This lack of concern, if taken literally, could prevent the kind of clashes which marred the relationship between Church and Academy. The Pontiff however wants more: "Science can purify religion from error and superstition, religion can purify science from idolatry and false absolutes" (M13).

Carbon dating has shown conclusively that the so-called "Shroud of Turin" is, in fact, a XIV Century artifact and did not wrap the body of Christ. This scientific investigation has certainly put an end to a long-standing instance where religion has actually purified science; we could say that religion was effective in criticizing extreme positivism and putting it out of history, that it stirred a lively debate on ethics and science.

On the whole the quoted statement of the Pontiff is a noble and daring one. His final plea for ". . . constructive relations of interchange through unity" (M14) is passionate, his concern for the future of humanity sincere. In spite of this I feel that he has a long way to go. There is a definite danger of direct collision with sectors of the scientific establishment, where memories of the stormy past are still lingering and ready to flare up at the slightest suspicion that the Church is dragging her feet. Before we go ahead we must dispose once and for all of the Galileo trial.

JOINING SCIENCE AND RELIGION

Holmes Rolston, III

"How does belief in a Creator relate to natural science? It is a question almost guaranteed to cause discomfort for the believer." [1] The author of this statement, Ernan McMullin, a Catholic priest and a philosopher of science, surveys the efforts to join theology and science over the centuries to find "tension almost from the beginning" and to conclude that today, as scientific "understanding has deepened, the signs of God's active presence in nature, once evident to all, have become equivocal".[2] If John Paul II ever knew this tension and equivocation, he has with the current message gone past all such discomfort and confidently, even comfortably, expects to join science and religion in a unified vision of the divine creation and the human place within it.

Like many conciliatory religious documents, the Pope's message uses carefully nuanced turns of phrase. The Pope is for: integration, collaborative interaction, integrity, unity, vision, depth, honesty, courage, critical openness, mutual interchange, growth, maturity, autonomy, distinctiveness. The Pope is against: fragmentation, partial perspectives, simple neutrality, shallowness, unilateral reduction, pseudo-science, unconscious theology, homogenization, unconsidered absolutizing of results beyond their reasonable and proper limits, self-imposed isolation, needless conflicts, divided community. Those are magnanimous and pejorative words, regardless of subject matter; everyone will be respectively for and against such things. But what does this mean operationally for joining science and religion? The virtue of statements of this kind is identical to their vice. Subtly composed, everywhere hedged with complementary qualifications, they risk minimum exposure to error, and this may mean that they offer little exposure to testing. Profound insights resist simple treatment; still, a theory should invite falsification. Let us test the Pope's claims against what others think, especially contributors to the volume in which the papal message is published.

Immediately following the Pope's message, Ian G. Barbour summarizes his lifetime of thought about ways of relating science and religion in terms of four categories: "*Conflict, Independence, Dialogue*, and *Integration*.[3] It is difficult to conceive of any two subject areas whose relations would not lie somewhere within these broad categories. If we use these categories to plot the Pope's convictions, we find that he is against conflict, and variously for independence, dialogue, and integration. He wants an "intense dialogue" (M11), and an "interactive relationship" (M9), while insisting on a kind of independence. "Religion is not founded on science nor is science an extension of religion" (M8).

When we try to pinpoint the logic of this joining, one is struck with the c's which occur throughout the volume:[4]

    –collaborative interaction (the Pope)
    –correlative unity (the Pope)
    –consonance (Ernan McMullin)
    –compatibility (W. N. Clarke)
    –consistent with (Freeman Dyson)
    –complementary (Victor Weisskopf)
    –compatibility, consonance, or coherence (W. R. Stoeger)
    –collaborative model (David Tracy and Nicholas Lash)
    –congruence (Arthur Peacocke)
    –complementary, hypothetical, cognitive consonance (Ted Peters)
    –congenial evidence (Holmes Rolston)
    –comprehensive metaphysics (Ian Barbour)

"Confirm" and "conclude," though familiar terms in science and logic, do not appear on the c-list above, nor does Karl Popper's weaker "corroborate."

Several c-words are disliked:

    –concordism (Tracy and Lash)
    –conflict (the Pope, Barbour, and others)
    –cognitive dissonance (Peters)
    –confrontation (Tracy, Lash, and others)

Comparing the disfavored and favored words, religion and science should be joined neither too comfortably close nor too combatively. Since "support" is frowned upon (McMullin, Stoeger), "confirm" would be too concordism. On the other extreme, confrontation is a regrettable legacy of the past. Conciliation is the hope of the day.

Also, we can add:

    –contrasting languages (Langdon Gilkey)

This last model is not denied, but is not enough.

Joining Physics and Theology

Many, perhaps even most, physicists today think that physics, especially cosmology, is compatible with some kind of monotheism. Freeman Dyson is explicit about this:

I conclude from the existence of these accidents of physics and astronomy that the universe is an unexpectedly hospitable place for living creatures to make their home in. Being a scientist, trained in the habits of thought and language of the twentieth century rather than the eighteenth, I do not claim that the architecture of the universe proves the existence of God. I claim only that the architecture of the universe is *consistent with* the hypothesis that mind plays an essential role in its functioning.[5]

Victor Weisskopf concludes:

The origin of the universe can be talked about not only in scientific terms, but also in poetic and spiritual language, an approach that is *complementary* to the scientific one. Indeed, the Judeo-Christian tradition describes the beginning of the world in a way that is surprisingly similar to the scientific model.[6]

A big surprise in recent decades is the anthropic principle in cosmology, summarized by John Leslie, who finds it perfectly intelligible to "draw conclusions from a fine-tuned universe"[7], though monotheist conclusions are not the only ones that can be drawn, and are not the conclusions Leslie himself draws. This suggests that monotheism is "consistent with" or "complementary to" physical cosmology, but not a conclusion commanded by it. Also, the monotheism suggested may be unorthodox. Frank Tipler offers us "a physical theory for an evolving God".[8]

Ernan McMullin has also gone past the almost guaranteed discomfort of relating science and religion. There is "*consonance*" between physics and theology, and "consonance here is more than logical consistency but much less than proof", though McMullin is chary of too easy an integration, mindful of the "hazards of the older natural theology".[9] W. N. Clarke finds noteworthy "the openness to, or '*compatibility*' of the scientific picture with, the theistic hypothesis"[10], and he too warns that this is only compatibility, not some further establishing of theism. I once wrote that the evidence from physics is "permissive or *congenial* evidence, nothing more."[11]

We cannot say: If P, then G, that physics implies God by hard implication, though we can say: If G, then P, that if there is God, then the world of physics follows, not as hard implication, but as a plausible world, a likely story wrought by such a God. There is a formal logical fallacy in backtracking from an observed physical world [P] to a hypothesized [G], but all science is caught in just that logical bind as it moves from theory to observation and back again: If T, then O.[12] Positive observations can at best corroborate, be consistent, congenial, consonant, compatible with the theory, although negative observations [not O] do confront and seem to defeat it. We begin to see the softer logic for which those c-words were groping.

The main issue seems to be how friendly is too friendly a relationship. "What one cannot say is, first, that the Christian doctrine of creation [C] 'supports' the Big Bang model [B], or, second, that the Big Bang model 'supports' the Christian doctrine of creation."[13] McMullin must mean that C does not imply B nor does B imply C by direct logical implication. But consonance is not independence. The two are more congenial; there is more than logical consistency. If, from the side of theology, there is divine creation, then the Big Bang cosmology is a plausible scientific account of it.

William R. Stoeger wants *'compatibility, consonance or coherence"* but is not sure that he likes it here.[14] "Even establishing a rough parallel, or consonance, between 'the beginning of time' in the Big Bang and 'the beginning of time' in the doctrine of creation . . . is very questionable."[15] That places him on the independence side of McMullin. Ted Peters is more bold and stands on the compatibilist side: "The Christian doctrine of creation out of nothing (*creatio ex nihilo*) is sufficiently intelligible to warrant continued probings for *complementary* notions in the natural sciences." There is "*hypothetical consonance*" between theology and the sciences, for example, "the possible consonance of this religious idea with the second law of thermodynamics and Big Bang cosmology in physics." Such "*cognitive consonance*" is "more than simple avoidance of *cognitive dissonance*".[16] In the vocabulary of Tracy and Lash, he is more a "concordist".[17]

Within the memory of most of these authors there were two seriously competing cosmologies: the Steady State theory, discarded since the mid 1960's, and the now favored Big Bang theory. Suppose that the Steady State had proved true? Would theology have been the worse? The Steady State theory posited the continuous but infrequent *ex nihilo* insertion of subatomic particles throughout the universe, and thus no absolute beginning. That theory also required the assembly of the light elements, followed by the stars, galaxies, the heavier elements within the stars, then planets, then people – hardly any less creation for the lack of an initial event. Nothing in Christianity implies the detail of the Big Bang theory; many other cosmologies are compatible with Christian faith in creation. Yet within the lifetimes of these authors, the Big Bang model might prove wrong and the now novel plasma cosmology, which like the Steady State theory supposes a universe without a beginning, might replace it.[18] If it did so, the search for consonance would have to start all over. It is difficult to envision any cosmology, however, that does not require creation of the complex out of the simple, more out of less, something out of nothing.

Meanwhile the Big Bang theory in one version or another is dominant at the moment. In that light, when these several scholars try to envision creation, they attempt to walk a knife edge of compatibility without falling on the side of too much or too little alliance. To change the metaphor, they know that the religion that is married to science today is a widow tomorrow, while the religion that is divorced from science today leaves no offspring tomorrow.[19]

In more prosaic language, this is what the Pope means when he claims that:

> Contemporary physics furnishes a striking example. . . [There is] a *correlative unity* . . . reflected and even reinforced in what contemporary science is revealing to us. As we behold the incredible development of scientific research we detect an underlying movement toward the discovery of levels of law and process which unify created reality and which at the same time have given rise to the vast diversity of structures and organisms which constitute the physical and biological, and even the psychological and sociological worlds (M6).

On the one hand, the Pope does not want theologians ". . . making uncritical and overhasty use for apologetic purposes of such recent theories as that of the 'Big Bang' cosmology" (M11-122). Perhaps he remembers that Pope Pius XII hoped, on the basis of Genesis, that the Big Bang theory was true and the Steady State theory false.[20] "We are not envisioning a disciplinary unity between theology and science like that which exists within a given scientific field or within theology proper." (M7) On the other hand he does not want to ". . . keep them from discounting altogether the potential relevance of such theories to the deepening of understanding in traditional areas of theological inquiry" (M12). He wants consonance but not concord.

Joining Biology and Theology

The conflict is in biology. The Pope notices, correctly, that discoveries at the molecular level have unified biology by finding common biochemistries; but evolutionary history is less evidently ". . . another impressive manifestation of the unity of nature" (M7). We know, of course, even before we look, that the physics of the universe is adequate for life. Here we are! A constraint on physical cosmology in any millennium is that it yield evolutionary history on earth. Any physics must allow for these biological appearances. From that point of view the details of microphysics and astrophysics, whatever they are, make no further difference; it is the biology that counts.

Creation refers to physical cosmology from the Big Bang onward, twenty billion years ago; creation no less refers to the genesis of life on earth over the last five billion years. Biology is not the focus of this particular volume, but no one can reach a "*correlative unity*" of science and religion without moving through it. At this point Arthur Peacocke, the only biologist among the participants, tries to see "*congruence*".[21]

Unity within biology is another world from physics, despite the fact that physics must deliver the biological world. Many, perhaps most, biologists doubt whether there are any absolute laws in biology in the physicist's sense: universal laws, formalized in equations and applicable across the universe. In biology there are only trends. Protein molecules and the genetic code are earthbound; matter and energy are necessary but after that their composition is as historical as it is material and energetic. If the rule that the best adapted survive is universally true, not only on earth but wherever there is life, it is difficult to frame this truth in nontautological form. Certainly on earth that truth does not deliver a very impressive biological unity.

Nor is there any easy consonance with theology. To the contrary, there is guaranteed discomfort. The Pontiff's hope seems born in physics only to die in biology:

> Understanding is achieved when many data are unified by a
> common structure. The one illuminates the many. It makes
> sense of the whole. Simple multiplicity is chaos; an insight, a
> single model, can give that chaos structure and draw it into
> intelligibility. (M9)

That the fittest survive unifies all the data perhaps; still, Darwin, upon discovering this, exclaimed that the process was "clumsy, wasteful, blundering, low, and horribly cruel."[22] Einstein said no such thing upon discovering relativity.

Most biologists are resigned to a sense of aimlessness, of wandering tragedy, of random walk. The physicist's talk of a theory of everything, a theory that unifies all, seems almost comic when one asks whether it would predict the resurgence of mammals after the Cretaceous extinctions. Jacques Monod in a celebrated exclamation concluded that: "Chance *alone* is at the source of every innovation, of all creation in the biosphere".[23]

G. G. Simpson concluded: "Man was certainly not the goal of evolution, which evidently had no goal. He was not planned, in an operation wholly planless."[24] Stephen Gould insists: "We are the accidental result of an unplanned process."[25]

Sir Gavin de Beer, in the authoritative *Encyclopedia Britannica*, has no doubt about the conflict:

> Darwin did two things; he showed that evolution was a fact *contradicting* scriptural legends of creation and that its cause, natural selection, was automatic with no room for divine guidance or design. Furthermore, if there had been design it must have been very maleficent to cause all the suffering and pain that befell animals and men.[26]

Almost all biologists have a deep respect for created life. Yet monotheist biologists are as rare as those who think physics is compatible with monotheism are common. The Pope's vision of correlative unity may eventually prove true, but it fails to face the reality of present cognitive dissonance.

When those in the nineteenth century tried to relate physics and theology they sometimes failed because the theology was inadequate. The present conflict also exists in part because classical theology is inadequate. Better relations between biology and theology lie in better theological understandings of the relationship between order and disorder, open-ended form and chaos, history and law. As in physics, we do not expect biology [B] to imply God: If B, then G; nor God to imply biology: If G, then B. But we do not yet have an unequivocal plausibility account of the consonance. Unlike physics, the unity needed may not be that of engineered design; it will require more autonomy, adventure, more shepherding through green pastures amidst the shadow of death, a more cruciform nature.[27] Perhaps these alleged negative observations in biology are more important for theology than the seemingly positive observations in physics. If we really want to test a theory, conflict demands more attention than corroboration.

The nineteenth century reconcilers had more than a theological problem; in the twentieth century we learned that the physics then was not ready either. Perhaps today biology is not ready. Is there any unity in historical biology, any "arrow on evolutionary time?" John Maynard Smith frankly says: "I do not think that biology has at present anything very profound to say about this."[28] If Darwin is the Newton of physics, perhaps biology yet awaits its Einstein. The full story in natural history remains to be told.

Dependence and Independence

In the papal message we read:

> The truth of the matter is that the Church and the scientific
> community will inevitably interact; their options do not include
> isolation.(M13) Theology will have to call on the findings of
> science to one degree or another as it pursues its primary
> concern for the human person, the reaches of freedom, the
> possibilities of Christian community, the nature of belief and
> the intelligibility of nature and history. (M10) Each can and
> should support the other as distinct dimensions of a common
> human culture, neither ought to assume that it forms a
> necessary premise for the other (M9). [There is] a deep
> awareness that the insights and attainments of one are often
> important for the progress of the other. (M3)

Neither, in brief, is a premise for the other; but the two programs are forced
together as they support a common culture. The way Barbour puts this is that
"both science and religion contribute to a coherent worldview elaborated in
a *comprehensive metaphysics*".[29] Christian biochemistry is an oxymoron,
because biochemistry describes how my arm goes up (the muscle fibers and
the brain synapses), but Christianity evaluates why (if the arm goes out to
murder or to save), and at this point there are contrasting languages. So
Stoeger says: "One can do impeccable scientific research without adverting
to philosophical or theological findings or principles".[30]

But there is a more subtle aspect of the problem. We cannot live
without biochemistry; we cannot live well without religion or its philosophical
equivalent. Though science is not religion, it may need or presume a
metaphysics; it may be compatible with some schemes of metaphysics and not
others. Religion cannot suggest the content of any science, but it can notice
the forms into which such content is being poured; it can also defend a
content of its own. Science is not God; science ought not to be God; one
can do science without adverting to theology, but one cannot live by science
alone.

The Pope wants collaborative interaction to insure that " . . . science
does not become an unconscious theology" (M14), but, in a conciliatory
mood, shows little inclination to criticize science with its false gods. Mary
Hesse as a historian of science is more aggressive:

> Scientific 'myths' of the creation and destiny of the cosmos . .
> . are stories of particular significance, as validated by a

powerful social institution, namely science; they tell us what a
scientific materialist culture thinks it is important for us to
know, the latest version of the cosmological 'facts;' they tell us
about our 'gods,' that is some kind of sanitized, mathematical,
impersonal super-force, or even perhaps the great 'external
observer' who creates by collapsing all the wave-packets. But
they tell us nothing about our history, our laws, our class
structure, our social ethos, except implicitly that these things
are mere chance perturbations, imposed on the classic beauty
of a mathematically structured reality . . . Scientific myths are
largely a construction of our own making.[31]

Conciliatory as a critic of science, the Pope is bravely confessional.
"Christianity possesses the source of its justification within itself and does not
expect science to constitute its primary apologetic." (M9) Those are terse but
wise words, and to expand what they mean we can listen to Michael Buckley:

If religion does not possess the principles and experiences
within itself to disclose the existence of God, if there is nothing
of cogency in the phenomenology of religious experience, the
witness of the personal histories of holiness and religious
commitment, the sense of claim by the absolute already
present in the demands of truth or goodness or beauty, the
intuitive sense of the givenness of God, an awareness of an
infinite horizon opening up before inquiry and longing, an
awakening jolted into a more perceptive consciousness by
limit-experiences, the long history of religious institutions and
practice, of the life and meaning of Jesus of Nazareth, then it
is ultimately counterproductive to look outside of the religious
to another discipline or science or art to establish that there is
a 'friend beyond the phenomena.'[32]

In a similar vein Nicholas Lash says:

I sometimes have the impression that some people suppose
that, the further we go in our discovery of grand unified theory
or of what went on in those initial microseconds, the nearer we
come to the knowledge of God. . . . If we read the first article
of the creed in the light of the second . . . if we take seriously
the Prologue to the fourth Gospel . . . we shall be brought to

acknowledge, as an implication of the Christian doctrine of God, that we are as close to the heart of the sense of creation in considering and responding to an act of human kindness as in attending to the fundamental physical structures and initial conditions of the world.[33]

The creative presence of God is an inference back from God's redemptive presence. The microphysics, the astrophysics, the biochemistry, the evolutionary biology – all the natural sciences- have to deliver Jesus of Nazareth, and those who have learned from him how to suffer through to something higher, those who, forgiven in him, are free in love and have nothing to fear. Constrained by their experience, they indeed are free to love science whether in confrontation or in consonance.

Notes

1. E. McMullin, "Natural Science and Belief in a Creator: Historical Notes," in Physics, *Philosophy and Theology: A Common Quest for Understanding,* (henceforth referred to as PPT) eds. R.J. Russell, W.R. Stoeger and G.V. Coyne (Notre Dame, IN: University of Notre Dame Press, 1988) 49.

2. *ibid.,* p. 49.

3. I.G. Barbour, "Ways of Relating Science and Theology," in PPT, *op.cit.,* see note 1, pp. 21-42.

4. Reference is made either to the authors of articles in PPT (see note 1) or to others cited by them.

5. Freeman Dyson, *Disturbing the Universe* (New York: Harper and Row, 1979) 251. Italicized phrases here and below refer back to the list of terms above.

6. Victor F. Weisskopf, "The Origin of the Universe," *American Scientist* 71 (1983) 480.

7. J. Leslie, "How to Draw Conclusions from a Fine-Tuned Universe," in PPT, *op. cit.,* see note 1, p. 297.

8. F. Tipler, "The Omega Point Theory: A Model of an Evolving God," in PPT, *op. cit.,* see note 1, p. 313.

9. E. McMullin, *op. cit.,* p. 71.

10. W.N. Clarke, "Is a Natural Theology Still Possible Today?" in PPT, *op. cit.,* see note 1, p. 103.

11. Holmes Rolston, III, *Science and Religion: A Critical Survey* (New York: Random House, 1987) 76.

12. *ibid.*

13. E. McMullin, "How Should Cosmology Relate to Theology?" in *The Sciences and Theology in the Twentieth Century* , ed. A. Peacocke (Notre Dame, IN: University of Notre Dame Press) 39.

14. W.R. Stoeger, "Contemporary Cosmology and Its Implications for the Science-Religion Dialogue," in PPT, *op. cit.*, see note 1, p. 242.

15. *ibid.,* p. 240.

16. T. Peters, "On Creating the Cosmos," in PPT, *op. cit.*, see note 1, pp. 273 - 275.

17. *Cosmology and Theology*, eds. David Tracy and Nicholas Lash (New York: Seabury, 1983) xx.

18. J. N. Wilford, "Novel Theory Challenges the Big Bang," *The New York Times*, February 28, 1989, pp. C1, C11.

19. H. Rolston, *Science and Religion, A Critical Survey, op. cit.,* see note 11, p. vii.

20. Pope Pius XII, "Modern Science and the Existence of God," a 1951 address to the Pontifical Academy of Science, English text in a documentary appendix to Robert A. Morrissey, "Science and Religion," *The Catholic Mind* 50, no. 1071 (March 1952):128-192, the appendix pp. 182-192.

21. *The Sciences and Theology in the Twentieth Century*, ed. A. R. Peacocke (Notre Dame, IN: University of Notre Dame Press, 1981) 264.

22. C. Darwin, in a letter to Joseph Dalton Hooker, quoted in Gavin de Beer, *Reflections of a Darwinian* (London: Thomas Nelson and Sons, 1943) 43.

23. J. Monod, *Chance and Necessity* (New York: Random House, 1972) 112.

24. G. G. Simpson, *The Meaning of Evolution* (New Haven: Yale University Press, 1949) 292.

25. S. J. Gould, "Extemporaneous Comments on Evolutionary Hope and Realities," in *Darwin's Legacy, Nobel Conference XVII*, ed. Charles L. Hamrun (San Francisco: Harper and Row, 1983) 95-103, citation on p. 102.

26. Gavin de Beer, "Evolution," in *The New Encyclopedia Britannica*, 15th ed., *Macropedia*, vol. 7, pp. 7-23 (London: Encyclopedia Britannica, 1973-74), citation on pp. 101-102.

27. H. Rolston, *Science and Religion, A Critical Survey, op. cit.,* see note 11, pp. 81-150, pp. 286-293.

28. J. M. Smith, *On Evolution* (Edinburgh: University Press, 1972) 98.

29. I. Barbour, *op. cit.,* see note 3, p. 42.

30. W.R. Stoeger, *op. cit.,* see note 14, p. 242.

31. M.B. Hesse, "Physics, Philosophy and Myth," in PPT, *op. cit.,* see note 1, p.199.

32. M. Buckley, "The Newtonian Settlement and the Origins of Atheism," in PPT, *op. cit.,* see note 1, p. 99.

33. N. Lash, "Observation, Revelation, and the Posterity of Noah," in PPT, *op. cit.,* see note 1, p. 213.

RELIGION AND SCIENCE IN AN UNJUST WORLD

Rosemary Radford Ruether

Pope John Paul II's address on the Church and the scientific community represents an important outreach from the head of the worlds largest Christian community to the scientific community that shapes so much of the cultural and material environment of the modern world. Such dialogue is long overdue and needs to be continued. Religion, as both culture and institution, has been in conflict with science since the beginnings of the scientific revolution of the seventeenth century. In other religious communities, such as Islam, this conflict also has a deep and unresolved history.

In a time when scientific technology is being pressed to serve a steadily advancing military system and an increasingly consumeristic society, the human community desperately needs a detente between these two aspects of its own life: between the community that claims to represent empirical knowledge and the community that claims to represent moral values and ultimate meaning.

In their conflict religion and science have passed through several models of relationship to one another. In the extreme form of this conflict, each has seen the other as false by its own criteria of truth. For religion, scientific propositions such as the heliocentric universe and the evolution of species have been seen as heresies, violating the truths of revealed knowledge. Science, in turn, has seen religion as superstition, as mystical fantasies of a primitive stage of human culture bound to fade away as the scientific method establishes empirically verifiable criteria of truth. Marxist scientism and some Western secular scientists still maintain this extreme form of scientific repudiation of religion. The conflict over teaching evolution in American public schools shows that some religious communities view Biblical revelation and contemporary scientific method as rival sources of truth about nature.

In the nineteenth century, German theologians, influenced by the Kantian split between fact and value, pioneered an alternative way of relating science and religion. Science and religion were seen as distinct forms of truth pertaining to different spheres and different forms of human cognition. Scientific truth was factual truth based on empirical observation; religious truths were value statements that defined subjective, existential meaning. The two realms were each true in their own spheres, and there was no essential conflict between them, once the schema was accepted.

The split between objective fact and subjective value allowed science to ignore issues of value, and religion to bracket the historical, factual truth of key claims of faith, such as the bodily resurrection. Particularly since

World War II, with its revelations of the demonic uses of technology in Auschwitz and in Hiroshima, such a split between fact and value must be seen as both questionable and dangerous. Science cannot afford to ignore questions of value; neither can religion afford to ignore scientific knowledge and its uses.

A new model of the relation between religion and science which has been gradually emerging in recent decades accounts for the subjective element within scientific theorizing. According to this model, empirical data have meaning only as framed in interpretative world views. The world views, once formalized into paradigms, give the most coherent meaning to the data at the time. Thus there is more of myth in science than scientists have been willing to admit. Science must appreciate the value dimension underlying scientific knowledge and its uses.

Religionists in turn have become aware of their ignorance of the world picture that science has developed. They need to be informed about this world picture in its many levels: molecules and planets, earth history and ecology. How can people of faith speak of Gods work in creation if they ignore scientific inquiry into how this creation has developed and how it works?

Out of these kinds of considerations a new dialogue of science and religion has begun. This is happening very tentatively, however, and without a sufficient sense of urgency. There does not seem to me to be widespread interest in this dialogue on either side. Most specialists in religion and in science seem to be comfortable living in compartmentalized spheres. This situation will continue as long as each subject is taught in school curricula and lived out in the Churches and workplaces without dialogue between the disciplines.

I believe it is not enough for scientists and theologians to carry out this dialogue on an abstract, intellectual plane as a comparison of their respective truth claims. Both science and religion are expressions of powerful institutional establishments. Both of these establishments function in an unjust world and profit by and contribute to the maintenance of this unjust world. Religion and science need to examine the social context that sustains them and how they themselves support an unjust world ideologically and organizationally.

The idea of the scientist seeking truth in a value-free environment simply does not reflect the reality of the scientific enterprise today. Science in modern society is largely funded by industry or by governments who dictate the agenda of scientific research. This means that most scientists do not choose the themes of their research out of a value-free, disinterested quest for knowledge (it is doubtful whether this concept of disinterested knowledge was ever an accurate account of the complex personal and social motivations that draw scientists into research).

It also means that most scientific research today is done to contribute either to industrial products that will increase the profits of corporations or else under government grants to contribute to military weapons systems. Profit and coercive power define the end product of much of contemporary scientific research. In this context the idea of scientific research as value-free ceases to be an ethical value that maintains intellectual honesty and, instead, becomes an ideology that allows scientists to compartmentalize their research, asking only about the solution to the immediate problem at hand, but averting their eyes from the uses to which their research will be put by industries and governments.

The Church has also been biased by the social and economic context that has supported them. Christianity and other major religions were shaped by a patriarchal and slave-holding world of antiquity, and also served ideologically to justify these social patterns. Although initially Christianity had a strong egalitarian impulse, as it became institutionalized in hierarchical systems of organization and drawn into an alliance with political power under the emperor Constantine in the fourth century, it modeled itself after the surrounding social hierarchies. Women were excluded from leadership. Slavery was condoned as an acceptable social system by theologians, such as Augustine, and ratified by canon law.

In the medieval world the feudal system shaped the Church institutionally and was, in turn, ratified as a reflection of the cosmos and the relation of God to creation. In the age of national monarchies the papacy particularly sought to make itself an absolute monarchy and to dominate both Church and society from this position. The Catholic Church never succeeded in controlling the states of European society and was often controlled by them. But with the separation of Church and state in nineteenth century secular nationalism, the papacy has succeeded in achieving such a model of absolute monarchy over national hierarchies through its doctrine of universal jurisdiction.

Too often the doctrinal and moral teachings of the Church have been dictated more by concern to maintain its own power than by concern for the authentic vision of the gospel. It is this perception of the Church as more attentive to its own power than to justice, truth, and love that alienated much of Europe in the centuries after modernization. After a brief period of respite during and after Vatican II, when the Catholic Church recovered some trust among progressive people, this negative perception is again asserting itself. Thus, although Christianity possesses the prophetic and ethical values necessary for critique of culture, it too often has subverted this vision of the gospel to the institutional self-interest of its clerical leadership class.

The splitting of mind and body, spirit and matter, that has informed both Christian spirituality and scientific Cartesian philosophy, has allowed both cultures to identify themselves with a male ruling class as the natural masters of the universe, the reflections of God or Reason. Matter or the flesh has been seen as the realm either to be spurned for the sake of spiritual purity or to be dominated and controlled. Women, slaves, and other dominated people were implicitly identified with this spurned or dominated realm of matter. It is this pattern of thought as dominating power that has brought both human society and its relations with nature into profound crisis today.

Both science and religion need a profound repentance, a turning around of their world views and their ways of operating, that will bring them into solidarity with the parts of the world they have hitherto seen as the objects of their knowledge and power. There is a need for conversion of men to women, of owners to workers, of rich nations to poor nations and of humanity to the earth.

The Church has the words for understanding this need for conversion, whereas the scientific community, with its divorce of fact and value, lacks the language for such transformation. But the Church cannot be an agent of the transformation of science and society until it is willing to be open to such grace itself and to become itself a more credible model of transformation and service to others in its own life.

SCIENCE AND THEOLOGY IN A CHANGING VISION OF THE WORLD: READING JOHN PAUL'S MESSAGE IN PHYSICS, PHILOSOPHY AND THEOLOGY

Karl Schmitz-Moormann

When Vatican Council II opened the doors on the world in its striving for *aggiornamento*, a fundamental change in the attitude of the magisterium towards knowledge coming from other than religious sources was initiated. This was clearly not an entirely new start. Obviously the Church and her theologians have known times during which culturally acquired knowledge was integrated into the theological interpretation of the biblical faith. But there is much evidence that the Church and her theologians were feeling rather uncomfortable when confronted with that kind of knowledge made accessible to human society through the work of scientists.

It is true that scientists themselves very often felt uncomfortable as well with Church teachings and very often behaved aggressively when facing the teachings of theology.[1] Thus, it is understandable that, when science was regarded as an intruder and a danger for Christians, it had to be rebuked wherever it menaced the traditional teachings of the Church. This attitude did not hinder Church teaching and theology from gaining insights occasionally from new theories in science or from facts discovered by science. But it clearly was the general attitude of the magisterium to strive to dominate science rather than to listen to science.

Thus one should not expect to find in the statements of Vatican Council II clear references to the world changes brought about by science. But the Council initiated a fundamental change in *attitude* towards the world of science. *Gaudium et Spes* recognized that the conditions of human life have changed profoundly thanks to the growth of the natural sciences (and other sciences)[2] and that science and human culture in general may claim their legitimate autonomy.[3] The positive values of science are to be respected, especially its search for truth and its spirit of cooperation. Moreover, the fathers of the Council expressed their regret that Christians, by misunderstanding the legitimate claim for the autonomy of science, have contributed to the widespread opinion *ut fidem et scientiam inter se opponi sint*.[4]

Unfortunately theology did not then enter into dialogue with science, a move which would have opened the doors to scientifically known reality and which would have begun a renewal of theology. In the Catholic world of Europe there is no theological institution whose interest is centered on the relationship between the world of science and the world of faith. The message of Vatican II has so far not initiated a dialogue that would bridge the opposition stated by the Council. John Paul II has addressed himself quite a number of times to the scientific community, recognizing the autonomy of science which is rooted in its quest for truth. The freedom of science to search for truth applies, according to the words of the Pope, to all sciences including theological research, which is to be autonomous.[5]

If one takes seriously these statements, one can only wonder why, within the Catholic Church at least, the dialogue between science and theology has not been more actively pursued. Apart from some personal and rather local initiatives there has been no real dialogue with science and no profound integration of scientific knowledge into theology. This state of affairs is certainly not due to restraints imposed by the magisterium, although the situation was different before the Council. If one compares the earlier statements of the Church as expressed , for instance, either in the Syllabus of Pius IX, by Vatican Council I, or by Pius XII with those of John Paul II one cannot help but be impressed by the change in attitude and in judgment.

In Vatican Council I the autonomy of science was mostly seen as a danger to be restricted. This becomes quite evident in canons 3.1, 4.2 and 4.3 promulgated by the third session[6] which quite vehemently insist on the Church's right to restrain the activity of human reason and the possibilities of human knowledge.[7] In 1950 Pius XII repeated basically the same statement restricting the role of science in human knowledge:

> It remains to say something about further difficulties concerned with the positive sciences (as they are called), and yet connected in a more or less degree with the truths of the Christian faith. Some thinkers are loud in their demand that the Catholic religion should make these sciences of the greatest possible account. An excellent principle, where it is a question of really ascertained facts; but what of hypotheses, based to some extent on natural science, which yet affect the doctrines enshrined in Scripture and in tradition? Here we must be cautious; where such conjectures are directly or indirectly opposed to the truths God has revealed, the claim is inadmissible.[8]

After Vatican II and especially now in the message of John Paul the attitude is quite different. Convinced that the truth is one and that this truth is the goal of both theology and science, although under different aspects, the dialogue between theology and science, between the Church and the world of science, is no longer considered to endanger the Christian faith. The Academy and the Church are seen by the Pope as ". . . two very different, but

major institutions . . . [with] histories stretching back over thousands of years
. . ." (M2) For the theologian to see in science a partner in the dialogue with
this world and not a subordinate to be dominated and eventually used, to
recognize the necessity of science for theology, announces a change of
climate that can hardly be overestimated. The message speaks of the
autonomy of both science and religion: "Each should possess its own
principles, its pattern of procedures, its diversities of interpretation and its
own conclusions." (M8-M9) There are no longer any claims of supremacy:
". . . neither ought to assume that it forms a necessary premise for the other"
(M9). But both are urged to encounter one another with critical openness
in mutual interchange, each one guarding its own integrity: "We are asked to
become one. We are not asked to become each other." (M8)

The message of John Paul II indicates that we must know about the
universe in order to speak correctly about God. He turns to Saint Thomas
Aquinas as an historical model of this way of doing theology, since Thomas
explored nature for its relevance for theology by his use of Aristotelian
hylomorphism. Important for our consideration is not the particular natural
philosophy Thomas exploited, but his conviction of the necessity of scientific
knowledge for theology: "*Nam error creaturas redundat in falsam de Deo
scientiam, et hominum mentes a Deo abducit.*[9]

There can be no doubt that for John Paul II present day theologians
are far from having realized a theology which sufficiently takes into account
the scientific knowledge of God's creation. In our schools of theology we
find practically no teachers who are able to understand the work of science.
The lack of the necessary expertise has in the past caused the formulation of
uncritical and overhasty apologetics using such theories as that of the Big
Bang. John Paul, by naming exactly this example (M11-M12), indirectly
criticizes his predecessor Pius XII. To appreciate the huge difference
between the address of Pius XII to the Members of the Pontifical Academy
of Sciences on November 23, 1951[10] and the current message of John Paul
II one must read both together. It is painful to imagine the highly qualified
members of the Pontifical Academy listening in 1951 to the papal description
of the universe and its structures even down to the atomic level. The
knowledge expressed there corresponded at best to high school level science
and the theory of the expanding universe is treated as if it were proven
beyond any doubt.[11]

Pius XII in his address recognized certain scientific facts: the age of
the universe as older than the biblical story allows, the evolution of the
cosmos, and even the geological data which indicate that all organisms on
earth had a starting point in time. This certainly was in those days a step
away from the attitude of the magisterium towards science. But it is clear
that the arguments were not based on an acceptance of the view which would

have been broadly supported in science. And it is also clear that the arguments were selected to serve the apologetic goal, that is, to prove the beginning of the universe . This seems to be exactly the kind of apologetical use of science we are warned to avoid by John Paul II.

This becomes even more evident if one looks at the arguments missing in Pius XII's address. While he praises the argument in favor of the expanding universe, and even names the geological evidence for the sequences of organisms, he does not mention the theory of evolution, which he had more or less violently condemned some sixteen months earlier,[12] although he allows for the evolution of the chemical elements. At a time when the evolution of the species was one of the best established theories – much better established than the Big Bang theory – this silence of Pius XII in his general description of the cosmos can only be explained as precisely this kind of apologetical blindness and lack of real expertise in the world of science which John Paul II denounces as the apologetical misuse of science.

If we read the address of Pius XII critically we are forced to state that science was used for theology without changing in any way the theological perception of the creation of God being explored by science. Science is only used to confirm the prior knowledge of theologians and not to change their knowledge. The most fundamental change in attitude expressed in the message of John Paul II concerns exactly this point. Theologians are not asked to look out for arguments to fortify their old positions, but to purify and assimilate contemporary cosmology into their reflections upon creation (M11).

Considering the vehement arguments against evolution by the late Pius XII, it is liberating and astonishing to see evolution not only not rebuked or silenced, but recognized as a fact. And even more, we are asked to explore what light an evolutionary perspective brings ". . . to bear upon theological anthropology, the meaning of the human person as the *imago Dei*, the problem of Christology – and even upon the development of doctrine itself" (M11).

This seems to be a revolutionary change in the description of the tasks of theology. If we take seriously the notion of evolution there will be quite a number of directions that need to be explored. If the world is an evolving universe we will have to consider the whole of creation as a process of becoming. We shall need to know if this process can be described as fundamentally determined, or only conditioned but not determined by the past, or if it is evolving freely. Whatever our answer, we shall need to understand the relationship of Creator-Creation in a way compatible with our perception of the evolving reality of this creation.

The Creator, as the one to which the *imago Dei* concept is oriented, must not only be seen in his relation to the created evolving universe but also as the one who expects humanity to participate with him in furthering the evolving universe on its way to completion. If we are to be able to take on this task, we will need to understand to what end this universe is evolving. Can we recognize by analyzing the evolutionary process what meaning the Creator intended for this evolving universe ?

If humanity did originate from God's evolving creation, then we must ask ourselves if this process has come to a standstill or if it continues. If humanity's future is open to the evolutionary process, if human nature is still changing, how is the humanity of Christ participating in humanity's evolution? Even more difficult is the question of how to understand redemption in an evolving world. How is the place of Christ to be defined within God's continuing evolving creation?

It is evident that questions like these cannot be answered within the framework of the traditional doctrines found in the manuals of theology. This traditional formulation of the Christian doctrine was perceived and expressed within the framework of a universe understood as a static reality. Even the teachings of Christ in his time could not make use of the idea of an evolving universe; it would have been meaningless to his listeners. But since evolution is now the best description of God's creation we have, we shall have to revise all our traditional doctrines in light of it. In any case there should be one evident point: in as much as through evolution new realities come into being which cannot be explained by the past, we shall have to accept the idea that the teachings of the past must be related to new realities which appear in the evolving creation process. The classical statement of Tertullian: "*Id verius quod prius*", can no longer be defended. Theologians, and with them all people, must accept that God continues to create – and not only to maintain – through evolution.

We are asked to reflect on these matters – among others – by the message of John Paul II. With few exceptions theologians, in Europe at least, have avoided these matters. In these questions the Pope has thus done something which the Church and theologians would not have expected: instead of restraining theologians from entering fields that are currently explored with only small effort or not at all, the Pope opens wide the door into this world unknown to the theologians and asks them to dare a new and a real dialogue with God's evolving Creation as it is explored by science. Let us keep this door open.

Notes

1. The roots of the scientist's discomfort are symbolized by the name of Galileo Galilei. For the aggressiveness of scientists one should look in particular at the more popular literature of the 19th century. The names of people like Jakob Moleschott, *Lehre der Nahrungsmittel –Fur das Volk* (Erlangen 1850), Karl Vogt ,*Vorlesungen uber den Menschen* (Giessen 1963), or Robert Chambers ,*Vestiges of the Natural History of Creation* (anonymously published in 1843-

46) indicate along with those of E. Haeckel, W. Ostwald etc. this kind of materialistic-monistic attitude, excluding any possibility of transcendency.

2. *Gaudium et Spes,* art. 54; see English translation in *The Documents of Vatican II,* ed. Walter M. Abbott, S.J.(New York: The America Press, 1966) 199-308.

3. *ibid.,* art. 56.

4. "That faith and science are opposed to one another." *ibid.,* art. 36.

5. John Paul II, Address to scientists and students in the Cathedral of Cologne, Nov. 15, 1980. Cf. as well his address to the Members of CERN, Geneva June 15, 1982: "The Church respects the natural sciences in their domain and does not consider them a danger, but rather an impressive revelation of the Creator God."

6. The original Latin texts of these canons are found in *Enchiridion Symbolorum, definitionum et declarationum de rebus fidei et morum,* ed. H. Denziger, rev. A. Schonmetzer (Freiburg: 25th Edition, 1973); English texts are given in *The Church Teaches,* eds. J.F. Clarkson *et al.* (St. Louis, MO: B. Herder Book Co., 1957). Selections from the three canons in Latin and English respectively (numbers in parentheses refer to the respective sources) follow: *Contra rationis autonomiam:* "Si quis dixerit, rationem humanam ita independentem esse, ut fides ei a deo imperari non possit: A.S." (1810); *Against false freedom of reason:* "If anyone says that human reason is so independent that it cannot be commanded by God to believe: let him be anathema" (69) – *Contra pseudophilosophos et pseudotheologos:* "Si quis dixerit, disciplinas humanas ea cum libertate tractandas esse, ut earum assertiones, etsi doctrinae revelatae adversentur, tamquam verae retineri neque ab Ecclesia proscribi possint: A.S." (1817); *Against pseudophilosophers and pseudotheologians:* "If anyone says that human sciences can be pursued with such liberty that there assertions may be held as true, even though they are opposed to revealed doctrine, and that they cannot be condemned by the Church: let him be anathema" (82) – "Si quis dixerit, fieri posse, ut dogmatibus ab Ecclesia propositis aliquando secundum progressum scientiae sensus tribuendus sit alius ab eo, quem intellexit et intelligit Ecclesia: A.S." (1818); "If anyone says that as science progresses it is sometimes possible for dogmas that have been proposed by the Church to receive a different meaning from the one which the Church understood and understands: let him be anathema." (83)

7. That these texts could be interpreted in other ways is, of course, open to discussion.

8. Pius XII, Encyclical *Humani generis* (AAS 42 [1950] 561-578); ET (New York: Paulist Press, 1950) no. 35.

9. Thomas Acquinas, *Summa contra Gentiles,* lb.II, cap. III. This text is even more remarkable if one considers the extraordinary force used to defend this position and the fact that it was directed against one of the most important authorities in medieval theology, St. Augustine.

10. *Discorso di Sua Santita Pio XII alla Pontificia Accademia delle Scienze, 22 Novembre 1951* (Vatican: Tipografia Poliglotta Vaticana, 1953) contains the full text in Italian, French, English, German, and Spanish.

11. This was certainly not clear in 1951. Einstein's theory of the expanding universe was still rather in doubt; confirming evidence such as the three degree microwave background radiation would not be discovered until 1963.

12. *Humani Generis, op. cit.,* see note 8, no. 42: "Etenim sunt qui evolutionis, ut aiunt, systema, nondum invicte probatum in ipso disciplinarum naturalium ambitu, absque prudentia ac discretione admissum ad omnium rerum originem pertinere contendant . . ."

THE MESSAGE OF JOHN PAUL II TO THEOLOGIANS AND SCIENTISTS COMMEMORATING THE THIRD CENTENARY OF SIR ISAAC NEWTON'S PHILOSOPHIAE NATURALIS PRINCIPIA MATHMATICA

Thomas F. Torrance

The fact that a papal statement has been published on the relation between Christian theology and natural science is itself a notable event in our times. It signals an important public step forward in the intellectual interaction between the Christian Church and the community of science, and in the search, not only for unifying coexistence through open friendly interrelations, but for a shared vision in the understanding of the created universe in its movement toward a completion and fulfillment which will not be overwhelmed by the forces of dissolution and death. In order to achieve this, more than dynamic interchange is commended, for some measure of intellectual coherence is urgently needed in which theology and science learn from one another. The unity to which Christians are committed in Christ as Lord of the universe is surely being reflected in the advance of the physical and life sciences, not only toward integration with one another but also toward uncovering the unitary rational order pervading the universe which Christians believe has been impressed upon it by the mighty Word of the Creator. The contemporary situation into which the papal message has been sent is one in which scientists all over the world are evidently more open to serious dialogue with theologians than before, and in which theologians increasingly look upon the astonishing discoveries of scientists as reflecting and serving the glory of God. Dialogue, however, is not enough, and so the Church and the scientific community are called ". . . to intensify their constructive relations of interchange through unity" (M14).

Serious interchange of this kind between theologians and scientists, now actually going on throughout the world, is reflected in the volume *Physics, Philosophy and Theology: A Common Quest for Understanding*, in which the papal message is published. In it Pope John Paul II points to the way in which the findings of philosophy and science in past ages, for example the hylomorphism of Aristotelian natural philosophy, have been tested and adopted by theologians to help them illuminate various areas of theology. He also adds: "Theologians might well ask, with respect to contemporary science, philosophy and other areas of human knowing, if they have accomplished this extraordinarily difficult task as well as did these medieval masters" (M11). On the other hand, since any meaningful interchange between science and theology within our common intellectual culture involves mutual listening and learning, Pope John Paul II goes on to ask

"Can science also benefit from this interchange?" (M13) These are serious questions to which I would like to offer a brief response.

Neither question seems to take into account the immense difference between the kind of science that the medieval theologians had to come to terms with as a potentially important resource, and the kind of science which is said by the Pope to challenge theology "far more deeply" than did the introduction of Aristotle into Western Europe in the thirteenth century. After all Aristotelian science was not Christian, whereas the science that stems from the seventeenth century and later had at least some definite Christian foundations. Hence our modern science ought to be rather more congenial to the Christian Gospel than Aristotelian science. If the former is found to be more challenging than the latter, may it not be because the theology of the Church has absorbed too much from non-Christian sources, and has allowed its thinking and teaching to be seriously compromised by them? In this event dialogue and interchange between theology and science today may well purify theology from error and superstition, but I believe that purification of this kind must be allowed to take place at a deeper level, in the conceptual structure of formalized knowledge. I hope this is what Pope John Paul II implies when he asks whether theologians today, with respect to contemporary science, have done "as well as" their medieval predecessors. I agree, however, that the deterministic and dualist conception of the universe which developed out of Newton's system of the world has not been very congenial to the Christian faith, but part of the reason for that is that it carried over into classical modern science too much from its medieval inheritance, such as the concepts of inertia and hard logico-causal necessity. These are forms of thought which the great patristic theology relativized or even set aside when it gave intellectual expression to the doctrines of the incarnation and creation in such a way as to reconstruct the foundations of classical science and philosophy, and at the same time laid the basis upon which eventually empirical science was to arise.

Contemporary science has at last been shaking off the rationalistic dualism and closed necessitarian notions of natural law built into it during the Enlightenment, so that it has really become a helpful ally to theological science, and is certainly not to be feared. Let me illustrate this by reference to three great scientists: James Clerk Maxwell, Albert Einstein, and Michael Polanyi.

Clerk Maxwell's belief in the God who became incarnate in Jesus Christ made him question whether the universe created by the Wisdom of God did really behave in the way described by Newtonian mechanics. The crisis came when he failed again and again to find a Newtonian mechanistic explanation for the behavior of electromagnetism and light. It was through allowing Christian thought (such as the understanding of interpersonal relations derived from the doctrine of the Holy Trinity) to bear upon his scientific thinking that he came up with the conception of the continuous dynamic field, to which Einstein was to point as introducing the most far-reaching change in the rational structure of science and our understanding of nature. I believe that science has only begun to plumb the depths of that conceptual revolution, for example, with respect to the refined notion of causality that it involved. The Newtonian concept of causal connections between particles interacting on one another externally was overthrown for another, deeper, notion of causal connections between particles interlocked internally with one another. This called for a new kind of "embodied mathematics" but also for a new kind of "dynamic logic." How much more congenial that is to Christian understanding of the fact that in the Incarnation the Word *became* flesh in space and time, which may be understood not in a static but in a kinetic way appropriate to what actually took place. But that is precisely the kind of scientific thinking that has been developing from Clerk Maxwell, through Einstein, and now with quantum theory. I think particularly of the way in which features in the behavior of physical light can be correlated with God's interaction with the created universe in such a way as to provide our understanding of it with remarkably illuminating analogies.

Following Clerk Maxwell's discovery of the continuous dynamic field and the behavior of light, Einstein overthrew the Newtonian dualism between absolute mathematical time and space and relative apparent time and space, together with the way in which Newton imposed upon all phenomena the rigid necessitarian system of Euclidean geometry. This development had the effect of integrating form and being or theoretical and empirical factors, in knowledge and in nature at every level of reality. The epistemological implications of this were quite immense, not only for science but for all areas of knowledge, although they are still far from being adequately appreciated. Einstein thereby threw overboard the notions of aether and inertia, and rejected a way of thinking from a point of absolute rest in favor of a development of the dynamic way of thinking adumbrated by Clerk Maxwell. The conception of the universe that followed was what he called finite but unbounded, which might be described by mathematical propositions embodied in the dynamic structure of space-time reality, such that if they are necessary they are not true and if they are true they are not necessary. Along with Max Planck, Einstein laid the foundations of quantum theory, but was soon to become very critical of its "classical" Göttingen and Copenhagen formulations, because his belief in "God" would not allow him to believe in chance. "God does not play dice," he said. Most quantum theorists reacted against him with the charge that he was lapsing back into Newtonian causalistic determinism – but that was far from being the case. For Einstein causal relations were relativized like everything within the space-time metrical field, which demands a deeper and more realist notion of causal interconnection (that is "true but not necessary"), again more in line with what Clerk Maxwell had demanded, which cannot be constructed in the old deterministic way. "God is subtle," he would say, and "he does not wear his heart on his sleeve." Thus Einstein used to speak of the mystery of the universe as the miraculous "incarnation" (yes, he used this Christian term) of an intelligibility in the universe which reaches out far beyond our comprehension of it and which we may grasp only at its comparatively elementary levels. However, perhaps what shocked many of his contemporaries most was his insistence that science has now reached the stage where it cannot be satisfied simply with describing the ongoing processes of nature, but must press on to ask *why* nature is what it is and not something else. That is to say, science cannot be satisfied with determining the laws of how nature behaves but must penetrate into the ultimate unity of those laws and find the inner reasons for them. Until that is done science will not be able to get very far in developing the unified view of the world that it needs. To reintroduce the question *why* back into the inner structure of natural or physical science was not only to reject the rationalistic dualism of the Enlightenment that brought about the damaging splits in our western culture, but to open up the scientific understanding of the universe as grounded in a sufficient reason beyond itself. Only an open and unbounded universe can be consistent and true.

I turn now to Michael Polanyi. More than the other two I have adduced he reflected long and deeply on the profound epistemological revolution going on in modern science, and showed how, far from being antithetical to Christianity, changes in the rational foundations of scientific method and knowledge have actually opened up the way again within western scientific culture for belief in the Christian doctrines of the incarnation and resurrection. His own thinking took shape in his early struggle with Marxist philosophy, in which he came to realize that the closed necessitarian structure of Marxist society is the social correlate of an obsolete Newtonian deterministic understanding of nature. At the same time he worked out a conception of the open-structured society which is the social correlate of the open-structured science. Basic to his position was recovery of authentic objectivity in knowledge in which truth is pursued for the truth's sake, but in which impersonal abstractions are a distorting imposition upon the truth. It will be sufficient here to point to two distinctive features in his understanding of science.

First, he gave primacy to informal over formal elements in knowledge. While formal elements in science, such as mathematics and logic, may greatly increase the range of our rational activity, formalization remains necessarily incomplete, for it can never supersede but must always rely upon informal acts of intelligence. Just as any dictionary definition of a term presupposes and relies upon undefined terms in that definition, so all formal scientific knowledge presupposes and relies on informal acts of apprehension in which we are intuitively in touch with the reality being investigated. Thus we always know more than we can tell, and our true statements bearing on reality indicate more than they can express. In other words, all our scientific knowledge relies upon implicit beliefs for which we cannot give scientific justification, but without which scientific activity could not proceed. And so Polanyi set out to rethink the relations of faith and reason in rigorous scientific thought in order to "restore the balance of our cognitive powers." This represents the full-bodied recovery in science of the Augustinian and Anselmic *fides quaerens intellectum* mentioned in the papal message.

Second, Michael Polanyi brought back into the center of scientific research the responsible participation of the person as the active rational agent in all acts of discovery, understanding, and knowing. As it is only a person who can think, mean, interpret, or understand, so it is only a person who can appraise the validity of an argument or exercise judgment relating evidence to an external reality which they seek to apprehend. It is only a person who can discern a coherent pattern in nature and use it as a clue in active pursuit of inquiry; and it is only a person who can submit the mind to the compelling demands of reality, and freely think of it as one is rationally committed to think of it in accordance with its nature. All of this does not mean that personal knowledge is subjective, but the very opposite, for it is only a person who can distinguish what they know from their knowing of it, and thus only a person who can engage in genuinely objective and heuristic operations. It was Polanyi's conviction that cognitive belief in a reality independent of our knowing of it and accessible to all people is the ultimate determinant of the scientific enterprise, and that common dedication to that reality transcending ourselves and deeper than our understanding of it is the ground of academic freedom. While the knowing of God, Polanyi remarks, is outside his specific argument, his conception of personal knowing opens the way to it, for taken aright, natural knowing expands continuously into knowledge of the supernatural. "Such, I believe," he once said, "is the true transition from science to the humanities and also from our knowing the laws of nature to knowing the person of God."

I have certainly selected examples of scientists whose thought is congenial to the Christian faith, and who have a good deal to offer in developing the interchange between theology and science. There are other scientists, of course, although much fewer in number than they were, who as avowed positivists are not sympathetic to the Church, and would decline to engage in dialogue, let alone serious interchange, between science and theology. Nevertheless, the world-renowned scientists I have presented do give a clear indication of how constructive relations between rigorous science and theology can be upheld and developed. But what of Pope John Paul II's other question: can science on its part benefit from this interchange? It would seem that it should, he says, and adds that while science can purify religion from error and superstition, religion can purify science from idolatry and false absolutes. I believe we must go further than that, and ask whether science might benefit from a serious *conceptual interchange* with Christian theology. Actually there has been much more conceptual traffic from theology to science, as well as from science to theology, than is usually recognized, for some of the most basic elements in the foundation of science have been derived from Christian theology. I think above all of the concept of the *contingence* of the universe and its rational order which points to an explanatory ground beyond it altogether, but which in the nature of the case science cannot establish on its own through any examination of natural processes in the universe, to which it is restricted precisely as natural science. Yet it cannot operate in the empirico-theoretic way in which it actually does today except on the assumption of the contingence of universe. *Nihil constat de contingentia nisi ex revelatione*, as theologians rightly say. This is where modern empirical science differs so radically from classical and medieval science or indeed from Enlightenment science, for as Einstein showed again and again scientific concepts and laws cannot be logically deduced but must be freely derived.

Let me restrict myself in answer to the Pope's question to two related issues which, particularly since the rise of quantum theory, have come to haunt scientific explanation in the physical and life sciences alike.

In the first place I think of the problem of *order* which crops up on the frontiers of knowledge, where physical laws become critical and everything appears to be chaotic, and where meaning eludes us. This problem is so acute that John Archibald Wheeler has declared that we are now launched into a new era in which we must be concerned with what he calls "meaning physics". The human mind cannot rest content with a chaotic state of affairs and must find a way, through some regulating principle, which will enable it to offer a lawful explanation of things. To fall back upon statistical theories of probability at this point is not good enough, for that way leads back into a disguised form of determinism. I believe that it is imperative for us to ask whether the chaotic conditions that disturb so many scientists today are not due, in part at least, to the inadequacy of our conceptual instruments. I think of the lack of an embodied mathematics and of a dynamic logic which we need for what Clerk Maxwell called a "new mathesis". It is here that Christian theology may have something to contribute to science through its understanding of contingent order, that is, the kind of order which, while incomplete in itself, makes sense only as it is completed from beyond itself in God. Surely at the frontiers of knowledge, where being borders on nonbeing and our normal habits of scientific thought are suspended, it would be right for us to allow the transcendent Word of God, through which the universe was given its contingent rational order, to bear contrapuntally, as it were, upon the disorder we claim to find in nature, and thereby let it come to consistent harmonious order through being completed beyond itself. That is to say, it may well be through a serious intersecting of scientific and theological ways of thinking that a meaningful understanding of physics can be found which otherwise eludes us.

In the second place I want to raise the problem of *chance*. I recall that when the Church in the early centuries came to develop its doctrine of creation in the light of the incarnation and the resurrection, it rejected all notions of chance and necessity put forward by the Epicureans, atomists and others, for chance and necessity were but the obverse of one another in a completely fatalistic or deterministic worldview. It was then that Christian theologians developed the doctrine of the unitary contingent nature of the universe with its open-structured notion of natural law coordinated with the sustaining presence and power of the Word and Spirit of God. They thought of the empirical and orderly universe as endowed with rational properties by the Word of God, and thus as continuously existing in a created correlation with God's transcendent rationality. Today, however, contingence is still a problem for many scientific minds, even after the departure of science from the closed deterministic concept of the universe. How is it to express within the framework of traditional scientific conceptions the strange kind of elusive behavior in nature disclosed through relativity and quantum theory, and through biological evolution? Here scientists have tended to resort to explanations in terms of chance and necessity – and yet they are clearly uneasy about it. Thus even Heisenberg felt that the behavior of nature is so subtle and refined that it is not to be explained through resort to "the couplet chance and necessity". Erwin Schrödinger spoke of "intelligible chance", David Bohm of "laws and chance", and recently Edward Nelson has spoken of "space-time-chance" – all of which clearly points to the need to rethink the notion of 'chance'. Is 'chance' merely a mathematical device, a negative sign, a cover for our ignorance, or is it something real? It is clearly too easy for 'chance' like the notion of 'inertia' to be mythologized as some kind of unknown explanatory 'force', appeal to which is a kind of scientist's 'god of the gaps'!

Is this not a state of affairs in which Christian theology should have something to say as well, and in which natural science may well benefit from interchange with theology? From the theological point of view there seems to be a need for science to think more seriously about contingence instead of what it calls 'chance', and to think of contingence as inherently, although very subtly, intelligible in its own right.   Clerk Maxwell initiated the fundamental change in the rational structure of science through allowing his attempt to interpret the behavior of nature in a more dynamic and less mechanistic way to be prompted by his understanding of God's activity revealed in Jesus Christ, the incarnate Word, through whom all things have been created and continue to be sustained.   The activity of God revealed in Jesus Christ is inexpressibly subtle, refined, flexible, variable, yet constant – that is, like what in personal relations the Bible calls "grace".   Surely the behavior of the created universe is finally to be understood in some such way.   I believe that the time has come for theologians and scientists to engage together in the search for a more refined and adequate way in which to express how nature behaves at its deepest and most elusive levels where it is not completely self explanatory.   If what we find at the frontiers of scientific investigation defies rational formalization through our normal conceptual instruments, then perhaps theology and science may cooperate in forging new instruments more appropriate to the behavior of nature as it has come from the hand of God, and as it is unceasingly sustained by him.

RESPONSE TO THE MESSAGE OF JOHN PAUL II

Charles H. Townes

Introduction

I find the message of John Paul II both eloquent and to the point. It will encourage and be welcomed by many scientists. Science and theology represent two great efforts to understand our universe and ourselves, each with its own perspective. The insights of each can help increase the depth of our understanding, and we need a broad spectrum of individuals who can consider both science and religious ideas with some sophistication. Thus, this statement is pertinent, clarifying, and timely.

My own impression is that the fields of science and theology are actually much more similar and closely parallel than our culture generally allows. This is, in part, because of a natural overlap in their broad goals; science might be described briefly as a search for understanding in terms of order in our universe, religion perhaps as a search for understanding in terms of meaning. Both take an all-encompassing view, seek connections between all parts of our universe, and hence if successful must ultimately overlap in major ways and be one. There must also be an inherent similarity between our understanding of science and of religion because human characteristics mold both of them; by utilizing all our human abilities they call on and are blessed by similar human capabilities and also have somewhat similar limitations.

Consider Faith

It is usually not overtly noticed that science is built on faith; by contrast, for religion, faith is right out front. But faith is necessary for scientists to even begin their work; scientists, too, must believe so that they may know. They must deeply believe that there is order in the universe, a kind of order the human mind can eventually grasp. Without such faith, we would be in a capricious world not to be comprehended by logic or repeatable experiments. This is why, I believe, science has particularly flourished in a Judaeo-Christian setting with its background of a real world somewhat external to the individual mind, and obeying the consistent laws of a reliable God. We cannot by logic rule out Bishop Berkeley's world, created only out of our own mind and thus with a rather arbitrary existence; only the scientist's faith can do that. Sometimes it takes the faith of Job to persevere on a scientific problem which continually eludes us and makes no sense on the basis of our best logical constructs. Even what we consider logical proofs are, we now understand, based on faith – a faith that certain starting assumptions are adequately self-consistent. Normally, a mathematical proof is carefully deduced from a set of assumptions which, if correct, allow proof of a set of propositions according to recognized rules of logic. But the mathematician Goedel showed that no set of assumptions can be proven self-consistent without a still more general frame of assumptions being called upon, a framework which then itself cannot be proven consistent.

Thus in a very fundamental way, faith is a necessary basis of science even though we are rarely conscious of it. In another culture, one based on a pantheon of gods who on occasion countermand each other, the faith in reliable laws necessary for science to flourish might be difficult; for us it is omnipresent and therefore overlooked.

Consider Experimental Tests

Our almost unquestioning faith in science comes from repeated successful experiences or laboratory tests which others can reproduce. We do not question whether gravity and momentum will bring the sunrise again in the morning; we have experienced the reliability of the sunrise too many times. Science makes more complex and esoteric predictions; these can be tested and frequently they are correct, but if not then scientific ideas are appropriately modified without much damage to our faith in science as a whole. In some cases, scientists cannot experiment under controlled conditions, and must only experience and observe. We cannot experiment with a distant galaxy, and have no hope of doing so even in the distant future of space travel. We can only observe, experience, and from this draw conclusions. In some phenomena closer to us, such as details of the weather, we experience ever changing and unpredictable phenomena over which again we have no real control but about which we try to draw conclusions. And here, too, our scientific faith is generally confirmed.

In the religious framework, human experience, our own innermost thoughts and emotions, the experience of friends and forebears, the experiences we learn about from history or the scriptures seem to me essentially parallel to scientific observations. It is with them and our judgment about them that we test our religious ideas and faith. Clearly, religious experience is generally more complex to reproduce or verify than are the simple laboratory experiments of science. In some cases an attempt to reproduce religious experience – or seeking a "sign" – may fundamentally negate the conditions necessary for its occurrence. Yet clearly our observations in the form of life experiences or knowledge of the experience of others must form the basis of our religious understanding or the validity of our faith, just as experiments and observations by ourselves or others form the basis of our science.

Consider Limits To Our Knowledge

The remarkable buildup of science during the eighteenth and nineteenth centuries produced enormous confidence in its success and generality, and a conviction on the part of many that in time science would explain everything. The power and precision of scientific law had changed the idea of determinism, i.e. the idea that our future is already determined to the most minute detail by the past and by inescapable laws of science, from a speculative argument to one which seemed inescapable to most scientists. The honest scientist Pasteur could only reply, when asked how he could be both a scientist and a religious person, that his laboratory was one realm but his home and religion a completely different one.

The coming of quantum mechanics of course completely changed our views on determinism. As science entered the realm of the very small, i.e. the behavior of atoms, electrons or photons, completely unexpected phenomena occurred which radically changed the laws of physics and the scientific outlook while at the same time affirming most of our past experience on a macroscopic scale. Similarly, examination of new realms of high velocities and of strong or large-scale gravitational fields required the development of special and general relativity with other basic changes in physical laws. These again generally affirmed experience of the past but completely reoriented a number of basic ideas.

Quantum mechanics was especially surprising. It not only destroyed determinism but also required objects to simultaneously possess properties of both waves and particles and behave in ways at variance with our well-developed intuitions about the physical world. The future is not completely determined by the past, but has a certain chance behavior which, though most obvious on an atomic scale, is quite capable of strongly affecting the course of our macroscopic world. To many scientists, this was so contrary to their beliefs that they struggled hard against such conclusions. To others this contradiction of determinism seemed like a welcome opportunity for intervention of a deity. However, the equations of science still can make no allowance for a deity nor any other hidden or otherworldly forces. In fact, recently there has been much additional research on whether the unpredictable aspects of quantum physics are possibly controlled by hidden forces. This research has been coupled with attempts to disprove the strongly counterintuitive quantum mechanical conclusion that matter, or even people, can coexist simultaneously in two different states or manifestations. But experiments seem to give a clear answer that these strange and conceptually difficult aspects of quantum mechanics are correct.

While science still finds no place for a deity to influence ongoing phenomena, and no place for the free will we almost all assume for ourselves, it has clearly demonstrated that apparently well-established scientific ideas can be wrong in the most basic of ways, and that some of our well-tested and useful ideas can mislead us. Scientists today are much more humble and cautious about the completeness of their understanding than they were before these jolting scientific revolutions. And there are still other changes, such as what appears to be a rather conclusive demonstration of a unique time in history – the Big Bang – which is quite contrary to how many scientists previously felt our universe must be. We now search for missing matter, a majority of the matter in the universe which measurements show must fill our galaxy, and yet so far this matter is of a completely unknown nature. What new surprise does this missing matter have in store? And are there basic new principles involved in the existence of life which are sill hidden from us?

Science is extremely powerful and broad in its application, yet clearly we have grossly misunderstood the nature of our universe in the past. How well do we really understand it now? Is it surprising that religious ideas sometimes seem counter-intuitive or inconsistent to us? Must we not also be extraordinarily humble about our understanding in the religious realm, and be ready for the possibility of profound changes in this understanding? In either science or religion, we see only in part, or through a glass darkly.

Consider Moral Behavior

It has been often said, and with much conviction, that science is amoral, directly involving neither ethical values nor judgement. I am not convinced of this. It is recognized, I believe, that some of the religious rules of the Old Testament were primarily instructions for a healthy life, and moral perhaps primarily in the sense of enabling individuals to fully use their God-given human body and powers. Today science provides some of these instructions for a healthy life.

But more thought-provoking from the point of view of ethics is the discipline of truth which science teaches and to a certain extent also enforces. A necessary dedication to reason, tested by reproducible experiments, tends to hold scientists to high standards of truth and objectivity. False reasoning or false experiments tend to be quickly challenged and tested by other scientists, and this produces real punishment either for purposeful deception or for self-delusion. Science progresses when scientists are open, sharing and carefully objective rather then self-deluding. Not that scientists must always be right; when a scientist makes an honest mistake, which is not infrequent in the process of groping for new ideas, the discipline of truth and association with other scientists generally makes a ready admission of the mistake straightforward and acceptable. To what extent this discipline of truth is essentially adherence to ethical behavior can be debated, but in any case it produces strong similarities to ethical behavior. It enforces values which are demanding, are not self-centered, and are in most cases beneficial to humanity. It represents a standard of behavior which most of the scientific community recognizes as essential for progress, and which has blessed the scientific enterprise.

Consider Progress

The extraordinary progress of science in the last few centuries, and the more-or-less steady acceleration of progress during this time, comes from several sources. These include a strong faith in science, an interacting community of scientists which tends to enforce standards of truth, to increase the excitement of discovery, and to encourage a sharing of knowledge so that each new piece of information and each new understanding can be used as a step towards further progress. There is at least some analogy to members of a religious congregation each of whom helps, enlightens, and inspires the religious growth of others. One can hope that thoughtful, open interaction between scientists and theologians within the right framework of standards can also catalyze a growth in understanding for both groups.

In the case of science, our collective growth has been remarkable and the accumulating power of science astounding. More than ever, humanity through science is becoming a co-creator with God. This has its rewards for us, but it also makes demands.

Conclusion: A Mandate for Learning

I have argued that science and religion are closely parallel and must somehow merge when understood fully. However, they are still somewhat separate areas, and at times quite isolated from each other. Considerate and open dialogue between the two can be expected to enlighten each and to find much commonality.

It appears almost inevitable that humanity will understand the logic and order in our universe ever more deeply and will be able to use it ever more powerfully. This magnifies the urgency for us to also understand the purpose and meaning of this universe, the focus of religious concerns. How important it is for those of us with some scientific or technical skills to understand and participate in God's purposes! And how important it is for religious leaders to deeply understand the context of science, to be prepared for revolutions in thought and possibilities, and to help give perspective to humanity's tremendous intellectual potential!

THE CONTRIBUTORS

Since 1961 Richard J. Blackwell has been a member of the Department of Philosophy of Saint Louis University, where he now holds the Danforth Chair in the Humanities. He is author of *Galileo, Bellarmine, and the Bible* (forthcoming) and of *Discovery in the Physical Sciences* (1969). He also translated Huygen's *The Pendulum Clock* (1986) and compiled *A Bibliography of the Philosophy of Science*.

John B. Cobb, Jr. was educated at the University of Chicago and has just retired as Ingraham Professor of Theology at the School of Theology at Claremont. His current interests center upon process thought, especially that of Alfred North Whitehead. Among his recent publications is *Beyond Dialogue: Toward a Mutual Transformation of Christianity and Buddhism*.

A Professor Emeritus of The Catholic University of America, **Avery Dulles, S.J.** is currently Laurence J. McGinley Professor of Religion and Society at Fordham University. He is a member of the United States Lutheran-Catholic Dialogue and was President of both the American Theological Society and the Catholic Theological Society of America. He has written fifteen books and more than 500 articles on theological topics.

Lindon Eaves is an Anglican priest and currently Distinguished Professor of Human Genetics at the Medical College of Virginia. He is president-elect of the Behavior Genetics Association. He has recently published the book, *Genes, Culture and Personality: An Empirical Approach*, and is the author of more than 70 papers on topics in statistical and behavioral genetics.

After his undergraduate studies at the University of Cape Town **George F.R. Ellis** obtained his doctorate at Cambridge University (England). He has been a Clerk of the Southern Africa Yearly Meeting of the Religious Society of Friends (Quakers). He is currently Professor of Applied Mathematics at the University of Cape Town and is the author of numerous papers in cosmology and relativity theory. Recently he was the author with Stephen Hawking of the book, *Large Scale Structure of Space Time*.

In 1978 **Fang Li Zhi** became Professor of Physics at the University of Science and Technology of China and he served as Vice-President of that University from 1984-1987. During the cultural revolution in China (1966-1976) he was sent several times to labor camps. As a leader for human rights in his native China he was forced to seek refuge in the American Embassy in Beijing during the time of the recent events of Tienanmen Square. Recently he was allowed to exit China and is currently pursuing research at Cambridge University (England). He has published numerous articles and books in astrophysics and cosmology.

Elizabeth A. Johnson, CSJ is currently Associate Professor of Systematic Theology at The Catholic University of America. She is a member of the United States Lutheran-Catholic Dialogue and serves on the Board of the Catholic Theological Society of America. She has just published the book, *Consider Jesus: Waves of Renewal in Christology* and is the author of many articles on the theology of God and Christology.

Professor on the Polytechnic Faculty of the University of Kinshasa, **Malu Wa Kalenga** is also General Commissioner of Atomic Energy for Zaire. Among many other affiliations he is on the Board of Governors of the International Atomic Energy Agency. He is a founding fellow of the Third World Academy of Science and of the African Academy of Science and is a member of the Pontifical Academy. He has written seven books and many papers in mathematics, nuclear and solar energy, and electronics and he is the publisher of *Emergence Africaine,* a Catholic intellectual journal in Zaire.

Cardinal Archbishop of Milan, **Carlo Maria Martini** is President of the European Catholic Bishops' Conferences. Former Rector of the Pontifical Biblical Institute in Rome, he is a noted scripture scholar. In addition to numerous scholarly articles he has published widely on themes concerning spirituality and pastoral care. Noteworthy are his interpretative readings and meditations on Scripture for modern times. He is one of the principal and very influential leaders in modern Catholicism.

Ernan McMullin is Director of the Program in the History and Philosophy of Science at the University of Notre Dame. His early research was on the philosophy of quantum mechanics. In recent years his interests have been concentrated on the historical and philosophical interactions between science and religion. Among numerous scholarly articles and books, he is author of *Newton on Matter and Activity* (1978) and editor of *Evolution and Creation* (1985). He has been President of the American Philosophical Association (Western Division), the American Catholic Philosophical Association, and the Philosophy of Science Association.

Carl Mitcham is Associate Professor of Philosophy and of Science, Technology and Society at Pennsylvania State University. His principal research interests are reflected in the titles of his two most recent books: *Theology and Technology* (1984) and *Ethical Issues Associated with Scientific and Technological Research for the Military* (1989).

With doctorates in both philosophy from the University of California at Berkeley and in the theology and philosophy of religion from the Graduate Theological Union at Berkeley, **Nancey Murphy** is currently Assistant Professor of Christian Philosophy at Fuller Theological Seminary in Pasadena. She has recently published *Theology in the Age of Scientific Reasoning*.

Wolfhart Pannenberg completed his studies in Systematic Theology at the University of Heidelberg and is currently Professor of Systematic Theology and Head of the Ecumenical Institute at the University of Munich. He has recently published the first volume of a three volume work on Systematic Theology (German Edition, 1988). He edited the epoch-making work, *Revelation as History* (1968) and has published widely in Christology and anthropology.

One time Professor at the Institute for Advanced Study at Princeton, **Tullio Regge** is currently Professor of Physics at the University of Turin. He discovered the new symmetries of Racah and Clebsch Gordan coefficients. He has published numerous papers in the area of particles and fields and in the theory of relativity.

Holmes Rolston, III is Professor of Philosophy at Colorado State University. Among his many publications are: *Science and Religion: A Critical Survey* and *Religious Inquiry: Participation and Detachment*.

Rosemary Radford Reuther is the Georgia Harkness Professor of Applied Theology at the Garrett Theological Seminary and a member of the Graduate Faculty of Northwestern University. She is particularly interested in the relationship of Christian theology to social justice and has written widely on such topics as racism, sexism, and ecology. Her most recent book is: *The Wrath of Jonah: The Crisis of Religious Nationalism in the Israeli-Palestinian Conflict*.

Together with his wife, Nicole, **Karl Schmitz-Moorman** is editing the scientific works and diaries of Teilhard de Chardin. He is Professor of Philosophical Anthropology and Ethics at the Fachhochschule at Dortmund and is President of the European Society for the Study of Science and Theology. He has published many papers and lectured widely on the topic of evolution in creation.

Thomas F. Torrance is Emeritus Professor of Christian Dogmatics at the University of Edinburgh and one-time Moderator of the General Assembly of the Church of Scotland. He is well known for his studies on the theology of Karl Barth and for his exposition of the physics of James Clerk Maxwell. He founded the *Scottish Journal of Theology* and is editor of the series: *Theology and Science at the Frontiers of Knowledge.* Recently he has published the book: *The Christian Frame of Mind, Reason, Order and Openness in Theology and Natural Science.*

For his work on masers and lasers **Charles Townes** received the Noble Prize in Physics (1964). He is currently Emeritus Professor of Physics at the University of California at Berkeley. He has published widely in the areas of microwave spectroscopy, quantum electronics and radio and infrared astronomy and, in recent times, has been an active advisor to the United States government on public issues involving science.